"This book will challenge you, convict you, and expand your thinking about the two great essentials of balanced Christian worship and evangelism. Read it to go deeper into your walk with the Lord. Read it as a refreshing experience for your soul."

—Roy J. Fish
Distinguished Professor Emeritus of Evangelism
and Former L. R. Scarborough Chair of Fire
Southwestern Baptist Theological Seminary, Fort Worth, Texas

"The day of compartmentalized ministry that leads to turf wars and unbalanced discipleship must end. The church desperately needs an understanding that God is One and thus our approach to discipleship must be holistic. In *The Great Commission to Worship* you will find a compelling argument that you simply cannot choose to worship or to evangelize, because the gospel pushes us to both and more."

—Alvin L. Reid
Professor of Evangelism and Student Ministry/
Bailey Smith Chair of Evangelism
Southeastern Baptist Theological Seminary
Wake Forest, North Carolina

"When Jesus responded to the query concerning the greatest commandment, His answer spoke in summary more than priority. In *The Great Commission to Worship*, this principle is unpacked by the team of Wheeler and Whaley, revealing that the Great Commission and the Great Commandment are closer than friends; yes indeed, they are as intimate as spouses. This work provides thoughtful, practical application for us to live as the Lord Jesus also summarized, 'I always do what pleases the Father.'"

—Dr. Ron Upton
Minister, Music and Family Worship
Idlewild Baptist Church, Tampa, Florida

"David and Vernon have provided a much needed addition to our understanding of both worship and evangelism. Beyond that, they demonstrate that these two elements are and must be inextricably bound together. This book is a rare blend of biblical insights and practical helps that will change your life."

—Ken Hemphill
Director of the Center for Church Planting and Revitalization,
North Greenville University, Tigerville, South Carolina

"Finally, a work on worship and evangelism that sees them as God intended . . . a comprehensive way of life instead of two competing disciplines. From their years of ministry and teaching, Wheeler and Whaley speak passionately and pragmatically that worship, evangelism, and discipleship are connected and complementary. They are mutual and dependent expressions of a vibrant walk with God. What a breath of fresh air."

—Mark Becton
Senior Pastor, Grove Avenue Baptist Church, Richmond, Virginia

"While most church leaders understand the importance of the Great Commission and the Great Commandment, there has been little understanding of their interdependence. *The Great Commission to Worship* takes these two biblical mandates and weaves them together from biblical, theological, and practical standpoints, developing a masterfully presented argument on the importance of a holistic approach to the Christian life. Without a doubt, this book is the most powerful discussion on the role of worship and evangelism available today. If you could only have one book on worship in your personal library, *The Great Commission to Worship* should be it!"

—L. Lavon Gray, Ph.D.
Associate Pastor for Music and Worship
First Baptist Church, Jackson, Mississippi

"As with a number of other biblical constructs, evangelism and worship share a symbiotic relationship: one does not rightly exist without the other. In *The Great Commission to Worship*, Wheeler and Whaley provide credible, practical insight to keep individuals and churches from wrongly exalting one over the other at the expense of spiritual maturity or effectiveness."

—Dr. Mark DeYmaz
Founding Pastor, Mosaic Church of Central Arkansas
Author, *Building a Healthy Multi-ethnic Church* and *Ethnic Blends*

"What an incredibly biblical truth: 'True worship will motivate us to witness.' Pastors, your whole church needs to read—and be changed through—*The Great Commission to Worship*!"

—Dwayne Moore
Founder, Next Level Worship
Author, *Heaven's Praise: Hearing God Say "Well Done"*

"Vernon and David have written a timely analysis of the balance between worship and evangelism. . . . The authors capture a holistic approach to worship. The exposition of *The Great Commission to Worship* is biblically sound, insightful, and relevant. I suspect this thorough investigation of the topic will become an important source for many pastors and a necessary addition to the libraries of religious institutions."

—Dr. Greg Woodward
Chair, Division of Music
New Orleans Baptist Theological Seminary

The Great Commission to
Worship

Biblical Principles for Worship-Based Evangelism

DAVID WHEELER AND VERNON M. WHALEY

Preface by Robert J. Morgan

B&H
ACADEMIC

NASHVILLE, TENNESSEE

The Great Commission to Worship

ISBN: 978-1-4336-7237-8

Published by B&H Publishing Group
Nashville, Tennessee

Dewey Decimal Classification: 230
Subject Heading: CHRISTIANITY \ APOLOGETICS \
CHRISTIAN PHILOSOPHY

Printed in the United States of America

3 4 5 6 7 8 9 10 • 18 17 16 15 14
VP

Table of Contents

131024

Dedicated to Dr. David P. Randlett (1938–2010).
He was our mentor, encourager, friend, and the perfect example of
what it means to be a Great Commission Worshipper! His legacy will
endure until Christ returns!

Foreword

Would you go back and read the dedication one more time? Thanks.

Dave Randlett was my brother. He was also my model and hero. His untimely passing (at least for many of us) has left a huge hole in our lives. You see, Dave was no ordinary guy. In fact he was quite extraordinary. I remember running into a former university colleague of his who was mourning his loss. She made a profound statement about this giant of God: "David was a man without guile. He had no enemies." Yep. That was my big brother.

As his little brother, I can remember in his early high school years he developed a love for music. He played numerous instruments: he was in the band and orchestra; played piano in a jazz band; and, to my delight he played the "bass fiddle" in a late-1950s dance band. I thought to myself, "Wow, what an awesome brother. I sure wish I could do all that."

His years at a Christian college in New England cemented a deep love for music. But not just any music. It was there he fell in love with sacred music. He served as a minister of music while attending college, eventually settling on a long career as worship pastor and professor of college music.

So, you ask, "What does all this have to do with a book on evangelism and worship?" Glad you asked. I want you to feel like you know my brother a bit in order to appreciate his love for these two important biblical mandates.

Worship is so much more than music. It is a lifestyle of walking in submission to God and walking with God. Yes, music certainly is part of the equation. But a lifestyle of worship cannot be complete without a life of sharing—sharing the good news. My brother lived this principle and reflected it in both his philosophy and his practice.

He taught the principles of worship to his Liberty University students for more than twenty years. One point he consistently addressed was the tendency of young worship leaders to see music and worship as a stand-alone discipline—separate from other aspects of the church. That is, young students often believed they knew best about "real" worship and that their assignment within the church was to control the worship experience independent of submission to pastoral authority. "What does a pastor know about worship?" they would sometimes ask. "Shouldn't he subordinate his deficient knowledge about worship to me? I know best."

Dave taught them quite the opposite. He believed that worship was a piece of the whole, but not the whole. And, that the worship in the local church exists to serve the mission of the church—never to control the mission. He got it: worship and the Great Commission are undeniably connected at the hip.

About a decade ago, Dave relinquished his position as chairman of the Department of Music at Liberty University in order to assume the role of Senior Associate Pastor at Thomas Road Baptist Church. Under the leadership of the late Dr. Jerry Falwell, my brother was able to influence the awesome journey toward Great Commission worship. One of his roles in this position was to direct the outreach efforts for our church. (Never going far from his worship roots, he also led the worship in the midweek service.) He modeled the tenets of this book.

This past year, Thomas Road Baptist Church (TRBC) leadership spent about eight months rewording the mission and values of our ministry. During that process, the question was posed, "What does a Christ-follower look like at our church?" It was felt by all that the mission of TRBC must be based on Matt 28:19–20, the Great Commission, and Matt 22:37–39, the Great Commandment.

Thus, our mission at TRBC is to "change our world by developing Christ-followers who love God and love people." It is no surprise that both elements of worship and evangelism are clearly stated in the document and that two of those values emphasize the thesis of the book.

One value we embrace is for our membership to live a lifestyle of worship. This is demonstrated in part by powerful, God-centered corporate worship. Another value is to lead our congregation to have a passion for sharing, demonstrated in part by intentionally developing relationships that earn the right to actively share the gospel.

I am so pleased that this new document was completed prior to my brother's home-going. He loved that our team developed these statements. He even carried a card in his wallet that stated our mission and values. They were precious to him because he spent most of his adult life leading worshippers to see that true followers of Christ are indeed Great Commission Worshippers.

I find it interesting that Vernon and David are writing a much-needed book for the body of Christ on a subject that was embodied in my brother. He would have loved to have written this foreword for them—they were his students—but he will have to settle for the dedication page as he spends eternity worshipping the eternal Godhead.

Dr. Doug Randlett
Executive Pastor, Thomas Road Baptist Church
Associate Dean of Liberty Ministry Training, Liberty University
Lynchburg, VA

Preface

Albert Einstein once claimed that only eleven people in the world understood his theory of relativity. One of those was a South African leader named Jan Christian Smuts. Smuts wasn't primarily a scientist, but a statesman—a brilliant one. According to his professors at Christ College, Cambridge, Smuts was one of only three truly outstanding students in the school's 500-year history.

As a lawyer-turned-politician, Smuts established his career while World War I erupted around him; and he concluded his professional life after the carnage of World War II. He's the only man to have signed the peace treaties at the end of both World Wars, and he's also the only person to have signed the charters of both the League of Nations and the United Nations.

Today most people don't remember Smuts for his political career but for a single word he invented. It was a term he coined in 1926 and singlehandedly added to the English vocabulary—a word used several times in this book.

Holistic.

Rooted in the Greek word *holos* (all, whole, entire, total), *holistic* means that specific elements cannot be considered as separate entities but should be viewed as partners in a collective system.

Physicians instantly knew what Smuts was talking about, and they popularized his term in medical circles. We can't successfully treat one problem without considering the person's overall physical and psychological condition.

In systematic theology, and in colleges with their various disciplines, and in local churches with organized and subdivided ministries, it's common for us to focus our passions on the various subjects or spheres that most interest us or correspond to our personalities.

But what happens when you cross a worship leader with an evangelist? Well, you get this book, and you get a holistic understanding of the purposes of God and the passions of life. Approaching their topic from two different perspectives, Vernon Whaley and David Wheeler meld their minds around one indivisible truth—the only thing more important than evangelism is worship, and the only thing more important than worship is evangelism. God has married the two, and what He has joined we cannot separate.

Charles Haddon Spurgeon, the Prince of Preachers, spoke on this topic from Acts 17:6, the verse quoting a criticism aimed at Paul and his compatriots: "These men who have turned the world upside down have come here, too" (HCSB). Spurgeon observed that, as we discover who Christ is, our own little world is turned upside down. And as we spread the message to others, the world at large is turned upside down.

Though Spurgeon preached his sermon in 1858, long before Smuts coined the word *holistic*, he nevertheless understood the concept. Magnifying and multiplying are too interwoven to cleave. Try to detach them and neither makes sense. Put them together and nothing makes more sense.

David and Vernon are both dear and longstanding friends of mine, and both have roots in The Donelson Fellowship, the church I'm privileged to pastor in Nashville, Tennessee. I can't tell how indebted I feel to each of these men, or how thankful I am for their joint project. This book is the overflow of two hearts—one passionate for the lost and the other passionate for the Lord. But don't ask me which is which. Theirs is holistic passion, and they spur us on to the same. Great Commission Worshippers, according to Vernon and David, are those who are so in love with Jesus, so committed to worship Him, and so devoted to obedience of all His commands that they simply cannot restrain themselves from telling others about Him.

That's the sort of holy people we must be and the kind of holistic message we must bear.

In the process, we just might turn the world upside down.

Robert J. Morgan
Pastor, The Donelson Fellowship
Nashville, Tennessee
Author of the Then Sings My Soul series,
and *My All in All, On This Day,* and *The Promise*

Introduction

A Personal Note ... from David

My (David) life radically changed as a seventeen-year-old high school junior. It all started one Sunday night when my youth leader gave me a copy of the Roman Road Gospel Presentation to place in the back of my Bible as a reference tool. His instructions were something like, "I dare you to share this with at least one of your unsaved friends this week!"

It just so happens that I was three weeks into a new dating relationship with a beautiful young lady named Debbi. One evening that week she came over to my house for a romantic night of basketball. At some point during the game the Holy Spirit reminded me about the challenge from the previous Sunday night. I admit that I desperately tried to ignore the impulse for most of the evening—all to no avail.

In the end I chose to obey, thinking all along that I would make a complete fool of myself. I started off by asking Debbi, "Do you go to church?" She quickly answered, "No, not really." At this point I was sweating profusely and shaking violently in my tennis shoes! It was then that I mustered enough courage to ask, "Well, you are a Christian, aren't you?" She again answered, "No, not that I am aware of."

At that point I invited her into our house where we could sit down and talk. For the first time in my life I began to share the gospel. Step by step we walked through the Roman Road presentation that I was given by my youth leader. As I recall I was so nervous that

I couldn't remember the difference between Romans and Revelation. I am certain that I butchered the presentation and stumbled through my words. Nevertheless, you could feel the Holy Spirit move as Debbi surrendered her life to Christ.

My life has never been the same! You could probably make the same statement in reference to Debbi. We were eventually married after our final year of college. I am not normally a proponent of missionary dating, but in this instance it worked out pretty well!

It has now been 33 years since that night when I was awakened to the call of the Great Commission. In that singular moment I was invited to join Christ on mission as a human instrument of His grace as my spiritual eyes were opened to a new world.

For the first time I felt like a real disciple of Christ, not merely a spectator watching Him work from a distance. All of this launched me on a journey to understand the purpose of the Christian life. For the longest time I argued that *evangelism* was our whole reason to exist as believers. Didn't Jesus say that He "came to seek and to save that which was lost?"

It was at this point that God brought Dr. Vernon Whaley back into my life when we became colleagues at Liberty University. Vernon is the Director of the Center of Worship. Over time, we sparred back and forth on the subject of understanding the purpose for our Christian existence. While I was certain it was *evangelism*, he argued for the idea of *worship*.

From my perspective, I had participated in thousands of worship services in my life, but none of them changed me as profoundly as the experience I had sharing Christ with Debbi and seeing her transformed. From my perspective, what good is it to stand and sing a few songs if the world is going to hell? Admittedly, I had a very limited view of worship.

All of this came into question during a road trip with Vernon back in the fall of 2007. Imagine taking two highly motivated church leaders and forcing them to spend fourteen hours together in close quarters. It wasn't always pretty, but it was quite effective. Not only did our friendship grow, but by the time we arrived back in Lynchburg, the outline of a new book was born.

A Personal Note ... from Vernon

David and I have been friends for years. We attended the same church in Nashville back when he was in high school and I was in college. We really established our friendship when the Lord led both of us to Liberty Baptist Theological Seminary. David teaches evangelism courses, and I teach worship classes. So, it wasn't at all unusual that we would travel together to a missions meeting in Atlanta. It was a bit strange, however, when David got into the car that day in 2007, that the very first thing he said, even before we got out of town, was, "Which came first, the chicken or the egg?" To which I replied, "What are you talking about?" "Evangelism or worship?" was his reply. "Oh," I said. "Are we going to fight that battle again?" We did.

As we drove down the highway, we thoroughly pontificated our positions on evangelism and worship. It was obvious, at least at first, we were not going to agree. For a short time, it even seemed we could not agree on some kind of common ground. In retrospect, David's reaction to "worship" was totally understandable (albeit a bit unscriptural). David had the unfortunate experience of being around some worship-musicians who seriously misunderstood their calling. They were all about the process, planning, preparation, and presentation of worship music, but they had little sense of obligation to evangelism. In fact, they resented the entire idea that "worship leaders should ever be called upon to share the gospel." They saw their job leading worship as too important. "After all, we lead people to the throne in worship," they said.

I had the unfortunate experience of being around a group of preacher-types who marginalized the mandate to worship and at best tolerated those who were obedient to the calling to lead worship. The Bible says, "Go into all the world and make disciples," they sneered. Never mind that these same men *never* once walked across the street to share the gospel with a person addicted to crack cocaine or ever stepped foot on a plane to fly to a region of the world that needed to hear the gospel for the first time. They were interested in church politics that exalted their reputation. They were definitely interested in maintaining their bragging rights for the largest church attendance (albeit the numbers were greatly inflated—*evangelistically speaking* their churches were the biggest in the region.) I wasn't too interested in dealing with the ego or arrogance typical of those in *this* kind of leadership (also an unscriptural reaction on my part). Obviously, my position and David's position—left unchecked—are unbiblical and would lead to serious misjudgment in ministry.

As for David, he had all the right answers memorized, or so it seemed. Usually I was the one on the defense as I sought to answer each one of his challenges. I usually had some kind of sarcastic remark after his righteous jabs. To say the conversation became heated is a major understatement. It was a good thing the Lord ordained for us to be together all day or we would have forever parted ways somewhere on the road to Atlanta.

Then it happened. One of us said, "Okay, which is most important, the Great Commission or the Great Commandment—to love the Lord with all your heart, soul, mind, and strength?" I don't rightly remember who asked the question, but neither of us could answer with any serious integrity. We tried, but in a few minutes it got really quiet. I think that is when the Holy Spirit began working in our hearts and our own individual dispositions. By this time we were at our meeting in South Atlanta and neither of us could talk about the issue—probably a good thing.

On the way back to Lynchburg we started talking again about the whole evangelism-versus-worship issue. This time we both began with the Bible—not disappointing experiences with a few misguided worship leaders or proponents of evangelism.

We began talking about the early church and the importance of the Great Commission and what they did to accomplish kingdom work. We discussed the issues surrounding these early disciples and how the Lord added worshippers to the kingdom daily. We investigated the motive behind their evangelism—love for the Lord. We began to talk about how these servants of the Most High God were in reality Great Commission Worshippers. Not once were they divided. Their motive was to lead people from every tribe, tongue, and nation to become worshippers of the living Lord. In the process they sought to win the world for Christ. Their motive was simple: they loved Jesus, and as part of their worship, they sought to obey His every word. By the end of our journey, we agreed that someone needed to write a book on God's plan for The Great Commission and Worship. In the process of our discussions, we coined a new phrase for those involved in biblical worship-evangelism: Great Commission Worshipper. This is a person totally and equally committed to evangelism and worship.

What This Book Is About . . . David and Vernon

This brings us back to the question: "Which is most important, the Great Commission or the Great Commandment—to love the Lord with all your heart, soul, mind, and strength?" This is the right question. The answer seems simple: "Both are equally important, and both are divine commandments." So, what are the issues? How are they resolved? How do we develop a strategy for evangelism that does not exclude our responsibility to engage in worship. How do we involve ourselves in worship without ignoring or marginalizing the biblical mandate to evangelism?

This book seeks to answer these questions and articulate the biblical mandate to be a Great Commission Worshipper. There are several prominent assumptions and issues to consider. First, "What is it that inherently drives us to evangelize?" Second, "What is it about evangelism that drives us to worship?" Third, "How does one define worship and evangelism?" Finally, when all of these issues meet discipleship, "What does it mean to be a Great Commission worshipper?"

This book contains 12 chapters of thought-provoking arguments and practical steps that attempt to explain what it means to become an authentic (reproducing) biblical disciple/worshipper. You may be surprised by the honesty. The following is a brief sample:

God fully expects all of His children to multiply! That is why
we are called His body. Just as your cells naturally reproduce in
order to sustain life and grow, we are commissioned by God to
do the same as the church. To accept anything less from so-called
believers and call it discipleship is normalizing disobedience
to God and tramples on the Great Commission! This kind
of approach is naïve at best and will *never* result in creating
authentic biblical worshippers!

The modern church has lost its two-pronged compass of exalting
Christ in worship and reproducing His kingdom through biblical
evangelism. The aim of this book is to help God's people recapture
their Great Commission calling and to once again be like the early
worshippers in Acts 17 who attempted to "turn the world upside-
down for Christ"!

As you take this journey with us, ask the Holy Spirit to teach you
the same lessons we learned. Perhaps at the end of our time together
you too will see what it means to be a Great Commission Worshipper.

CHAPTER 1

The Mandate of Worship and the Great Commission

Our great object of glorifying God is to be mainly achieved by the winning of souls.

Charles Spurgeon[1]

As discussed in the introduction, the concept of this book was born out of the tension that exists between the call to be a worshipper of Christ and how that expression is lived out as a participant of the Great Commission. In most cases, Christians will admit their need to worship, but they will do so to the exclusion of becoming radical and passionate followers of Christ. They are not willing to bypass their fears and share their faith with a family member, neighbor, or friend who is a nonbeliever.

Based on the rapid decline in evangelism statistics,[2] the sad part is that so-called believers appear to be content with this disconnect

---

[1] Charles H. Spurgeon, *Lectures to My Students* (Grand Rapids, MI: Zondervan, 1954), 337.

[2] The following statistics are a little dated, but as a point of clarification they show a little bit of the story related to the decline in church statistics. Please note

in reference to their faith, thus allowing for outward expressions of worship with little regard to what it means to be a multiplying disciple of Christ. After generations of allowing this anemic expression of worship to exist with little or no challenge from Christian leaders, the result has been the normalizing of an impotent faith that ignores the Great Commission in favor of reducing worship to an emotional act of personal expression.

If you doubt this statement, then attend a Christian concert and watch how believers respond to the show. Regardless of the musical style, you will see many Christians boldly stand with their hands raised high or possibly laughing and clapping with great approval. In some cases, there will be jumping, running, or lying prostrate on the ground. There is nothing inherently wrong with this type of freedom in worship. Christians should (after all) enjoy their faith, but it remains to be seen whether this same boldness is transferred to daily living out one's faith with unbelievers as "fishers of men" (Matt 14:19).

Based on more than 30 years of observing the church as a university and seminary professor, pastor, and evangelist, to me it is obvious

---

the following: "The Combined Membership of Protestant Churches over the Last Ten Years": While the US population increased 11.4%, church membership declined 9.5%; that is an increase of 24,153,000 people but a decrease of 4,498,242 church members. Evangelical churches have failed to gain an additional *two* percent of the population over the past 50 years. No county in America has a greater percentage of churched persons today than a decade ago. Over half of all churches in an average year do not add one new member through "conversion growth." In 1900, there were 27 churches for every 10,000 Americans; in 1950, there were 17 churches for every 10,000 Americans; in 1996, there were only 11 churches for every 10,000 Americans. North America is the ONLY continent where Christianity is NOT growing. Church attendance has declined approximately 10% (plus) over the last decade. Churches are closing down at alarming rates: We lose 72 churches (of all kinds) per week or 10.27 per day; we gain 24 churches per week or 3.42 per day; that is a net loss of 48 churches per week or 6.85 per day. The United States is the largest post-Christian nation on earth and the third largest unchurched nation. By sheer outrageous numbers, our supposed Christian nation LEADS the world in every category of violent and domestic crime and social decay. Unfortunately, these social indicators are the exact same in the church as outside; therefore, the church is having NO significant effect on American behavior. Used by permission as compiled into a presentation by the North American Mission Board of the Southern Baptist Convention, 1999.

there is a huge disconnect between the biblical understandings of worship and evangelism. If not addressed in an honest manner, this false dichotomy will continue to stifle the influence of the church in a world that is seeking spiritual answers.

The purpose of this book is to address this most basic issue of interpretation in reference to worship and evangelism and how they impact our obedience to the Great Commission. Should they be treated as two separate concepts or should they be lived out as unified expressions of obedience as we seek to multiply the kingdom of God?

The Discussion Begins . . .

A few years ago I was invited to submit two chapters for the book *Innovate Church*.[3] The first chapter was titled, "Back to Basics in Strategic Planning."[4] I freely admit that my bias as a professor of evangelism was to reestablish evangelism as the main priority of the church without apology or confusion. In my passion to prove a point, I may have overstated the issue. Here is a brief snapshot of what was printed:

> Another misunderstanding is that evangelism is only one of several tasks that the church must complete. Narrowly understood, that could be a true statement. However, when evangelism is properly and intricately understood in terms of worship, discipleship, prayer, missions, fellowship, and ministry, it is no longer defined in such narrow expressions. For instance, proper discipleship is never complete until the person being discipled multiplies their witness consistently into those who do not know Christ.
>
> In addition, evangelism is usually thought of in the narrowest of terms as simply sharing the right information. However, while it is important to verify the proper information, that is only half of the message and ignores consideration of the relational and social expressions. In other words, it is impossible to divorce

---

[3] Jonathan Falwell, general editor, *Innovate Church* (Nashville: B&H, 2008).
[4] Ibid., 117ff.

Jesus' message from the Person He represented. Therefore, true
evangelism must always embrace the whole being in both words
and deeds. Anything less will normally result in dry and lifeless
orthodoxy or liberalism

The challenge is that most church leaders are unwilling
to admit that evangelism should be the main priority of the
body. Could it be that they are simply intimidated by the task,
or maybe they do not understand the holistic connection of
evangelism with every other responsibility of the Church? The
problem is that we tend to ignore those things for which we
do not attach intentionality. Quite simply, it is easier and less
intimidating to maintain the organizational assignments of the
church, than it is to embrace the call of Christ who Himself
"came to seek and to save those who are lost."

In addition, most people never consider that the Bible is
primarily a book about evangelism. You may be asking how
this can be? Let's think about it: if you take the message
of redemption out of Scripture, what is left? A proper
understanding of evangelism must include both the act
of sharing redemption, as well as being the message itself.
Therefore, assuming that Jesus' main purpose in coming to the
world was to provide redemption, is it not logical to assume
that His church should also prioritize the sharing of that same
redemptive message.

As long as Satan is allowed to minimize evangelism in the
eyes of the body and to divorce it from the call of the church,
the Great Commission will continue to suffer. For the sake
of biblical multiplication, it is imperative that the Church
understands evangelism in the broadest sense. Evangelism,
properly understood, must be reestablished as the main purpose
of the Church, not merely as one of numerous functions.[5]

While I still believe that evangelism is being seriously overlooked
as a responsibility in many congregations and the "church" in general,
I now realize that a large part of living out our faith "incarnationally"

---

[5] Ibid., 120–22.

is to be interpreted through the lens of worship. This is not to say, however, that evangelism should be minimized. To the contrary, it must be the catalyst that ignites a holistic lifestyle of worship.

It is like being back in elementary school. I remember building elaborate volcanoes out of modeling clay. We used baking soda and vinegar to signify a volcanic eruption. After placing several tablespoons of baking soda into the volcano, you simply added a small amount of vinegar and the fun was soon to follow!

It is the same with evangelism as it relates to the other functions of the church (fellowship, ministry, etc.), as we attempt to live out a lifestyle of worship. Evangelism is like the vinegar that ignites the dormant baking soda. While the soda has the potential of sustaining a great eruption, it is powerless without the vinegar. The same is true if we interpret evangelism as a mere task of the church.

This is a key issue. For instance, I spoke at a conference recently where I presented the idea that "evangelism *is* the purpose of the church" by placing it on a power point slide and strategically offered no explanation. Admittedly, I did this in hopes of soliciting a response from the crowd of church leaders. Trust me. It worked!

Before I could get settled into my teaching position, hands were raised and objections flew like large hailstones in West Texas! How could this be? After all, in their strong opinion, worship was the "main" purpose of the church! To them, evangelism, while important, was merely one of many tasks such as discipleship and ministry. What I thought would be a ten-minute discussion lasted more than an hour!

In response, I asked the leaders a simple question that must always be considered when approaching this subject: "Can a person be a true worshipper in a biblical sense if they are not redeemed?" Of course the answer was "no." I explained, therefore, that a person must be "evangelized" before they can become a biblical "worshipper."

Thus evangelism and worship have a unique relationship. I also pointed out that many times in Scripture it appears that while God is always our object of worship, the concept of obtaining salvation (evangelism) appears to be the motivation. As it says in Ps 3:8 (NKJV), "Salvation belongs to the LORD; Your blessing be upon Your people!"

What Is the Answer?

Consider what Abraham states in Gen 22:5 (NKJV):

> And Abraham said to his young men, "Stay here with the
> donkey; the lad and I will go yonder and *worship*, and we will
> come back to you."

The context of this passage occurred after Abraham was called
by God to surrender up Isaac as an offering on Mount Moriah.
This statement was the culmination of a three-day journey where
Abraham explained his actions by using the concept of *worship*.

Outside of the biblical arena, Abraham's actions would appear
to be that of a lunatic or a mad man. After all, how could anyone
rationalize even thinking about killing their child and call it *worship*?

Nevertheless, this is the term that was used. Why? It is because
worship is not an event or something we do *for* God. Rather it is an
act of unbridled obedience even when rational explanations are hard
to find!

Think about it. Abraham did not possess a guitar, piano, or any
type of musical instrument that we might associate with the idea of
worship. All he had to give to God was his full obedience, even if it
meant taking the life of his most precious earthly possession—Isaac.

Maybe that is what Jesus means by what He states in Matt 10:34–
39 (NKJV):

> "Do not think that I came to bring peace on earth. I did not
> come to bring peace but a sword. For I have come to 'set a man
> against his father, a daughter against her mother, and a daughter-
> in-law against her mother-in-law'; and 'a man's enemies will be
> those of his own household.' He who loves father or mother
> more than Me is not worthy of Me. And he who loves son or
> daughter more than Me is not worthy of Me. And he who does
> not take his cross and follow after Me is not worthy of Me. He
> who finds his life will lose it, and he who loses his life for My
> sake will find it."

Therefore, understanding the concept of worship as living an obedient life is essential to grasping the connection between worship and its relationship to evangelism and the Great Commission. If the heartbeat of worship is obedience, then it is impossible to be a true worshipper without being directly involved in the command of evangelism as expressed in Acts 1:8.

I have to admit that since my earlier writings in the *Innovate Church* book, I have come to the conclusion that it may be an overstatement to declare that evangelism is the "purpose" of the church. Actually, the eternal "purpose" of the church is to glorify God in all we do as we live out our daily lives. Since the Christian life is meant to be an open invitation to join Christ "on mission" as obedient multiplying believers, evangelism and worship are both hatched from the same egg. Ultimately, it is impossible to claim one without the other.

Understanding Evangelism and Worship

If the concepts of evangelism and worship have been misinterpreted and misapplied over time, one of the best ways to correct this is to address several common misconceptions related to evangelism and worship.

Common Misconceptions of Evangelism

1. **Evangelism is a choice**. It is generally accepted in Christian circles that the majority of believers rarely share their faith with another unsaved person. I have noticed this in my graduate-level evangelism classes. By a simple show of hands, well over half of the students will admit that they rarely share their faith with an unsaved person. One of the contributing factors is that evangelism is taught as an individual choice rather than a biblical command. This is misleading and dangerous in reference to the Great Commission. Consider what Jesus says in Acts 1:8 (NKJV): "But you shall receive power when the Holy Spirit has come upon you; and you shall be witnesses to Me in

Jerusalem, and in all Judea and Samaria, and to the end of the earth." The phrase "you shall be witnesses" is written as a direct command of Christ. The aim is to mobilize His disciples into the world to fulfill His earlier promise as recorded in Mark 1:17 (NKJV): "Follow Me, and I will make you become fishers of men."

2. **Just passing on information.** There are hundreds of ways to share Christ effectively with an unbeliever. In doing so, one must remember that evangelism is not just sharing the right biblical information. As I always tell my classes, "You cannot divorce Jesus' message from the life He lived." This simply means that Jesus not only shared the truth in word; He also embodied that same truth through a consistent lifestyle. While it is very important to share the correct biblical knowledge related to salvation, always remember that the knowledge you share is validated to the world through a consistent testimony of a changed life.

3. **A spiritual gift**. Contrary to what many people believe in the church, evangelism is not listed as a spiritual gift in Scripture. While some people may have talents that aid in becoming more natural at evangelism, the call to evangelize is meant for the entire church. It is not reserved for a selected few soldiers. Think about it: the word for evangelism literally means "good news" or the "message." The problem is that most people define evangelism as merely sharing the good news (a verb), when actually evangelism *is* the good news (a noun). Our problem with evangelism is that we define it by the action, not the nature or essence of the action. At its core, evangelism is the "good news" of Christ and therefore must be embraced as a lifestyle by every Christ-follower.

4. **Just something you do.** Evangelism must never be minimized to something you perform as a duty to God. Rather, like breathing, it should be an involuntary response to naturally share Christ whenever possible. In short, evangelism is the essence of who you are as you walk through daily life. It is the consistent and natural overflow of a deep and abiding relationship with Christ.

5. **In competition with discipleship**. I often hear people espousing the tenets of discipleship over the call to evangelize. They often

minimize evangelism and use phrases such as "I am a disciple maker, not an evangelist." This may sound good, but it is biblically incorrect. The truth is that evangelism and discipleship are dependent on each other. While intentional evangelism that leads to a spiritual conversion always precedes the process of discipleship, neither process is complete until the one who is being discipled learns to multiply his witness through sharing Christ with unsaved people. Possessing a genuine passion for biblical multiplication through evangelism is a key indicator when evaluating spiritual maturity.

6. **Based on your personality**. Some people believe that evangelism is only reserved for "type A" personalities. Nothing could be further from the truth. Evangelism is a biblical mandate to be fulfilled through all types of people. Whether you are shy or outgoing, remember that every Christian is responsible to the call of evangelism.

7. **The same as "missions."** The word *evangelism* has lost its distinctiveness and importance to the church over the past 25 years as many people have replaced it with the concept of "missions." The essential nature and expression of evangelism is the passionate proclamation of the message of the gospel to the end that people will be redeemed as they trust Christ and His saving work at the cross to receive forgiveness and eternal life. On the other hand, missions is a transcultural enterprise in which the gospel message is taken into another culture at home or overseas (Acts 1:8). It always has evangelism at its heart. If the pursuit of missions drives evangelism to the point that sharing the gospel message is secondary, then both expressions lose their biblical focus. Evangelism must be the purpose and driving force of all missions. It is impossible to do authentic missions without intentionally doing evangelism.

8. **Acting arrogant or superior.** First Peter 5:6 says, "Humble yourselves, therefore, under God's mighty hand, that he may lift you up in due time" (NIV). The key to effective evangelism is a well-prepared, obedient, loving, and humble heart for God. A "know it all" and "cocky" attitude will always hinder the effectiveness of evangelism.

9. **Meant to be silenced by fear**. In 2 Tim 1:7–8, the apostle Paul states, "For God did not give us a spirit of timidity [fear], but a spirit of power, of love and of self-discipline. So do not be ashamed to testify about our Lord" (NIV). According to Scripture, appropriate fear is rational in certain situations, but this should not apply to the task of evangelism.

10. **A theological dilemma.** Some people try to use theological constructs to ignore the Great Commission. Because of unbiblical inferences related to the doctrine of election, many contemporary ministers are ignoring their responsibility to be active in evangelism. The same is true when liberal theologians compromise the authority of Scripture. In many cases humility and obedience are replaced by theological superiority and a critical spirit that is detrimental to evangelism. In short, theology without evangelism is not Christian theology at all. At the same time, evangelism without proper theology is equally as dangerous to the Great Commission.[6]

11. **Prayer by itself**. It is a misconception to equate prayer alone as an act of evangelism. Does this mean that prayer is not essential to the process of evangelism? Absolutely not! There is no way that a person could ever be effective in evangelism without possessing a deep and abiding relationship to God in prayer. However, to assume that prayer by itself equals evangelism stops short of the desired target. Actually, it has been my experience that when people begin to pray earnestly for their unsaved friends and family, their burden is increased and the usual result is to be propelled into the field to boldly share Christ with those in need.

12. **Church planting by itself.** Because there will probably be numerous church planters who will read this book, it needs to be stated that church planting alone is not necessarily an act of evangelism. In fact, after years of working with church planters, I am sometimes alarmed by the overemphasis on worship and discipleship to the exclusion of evangelism that leads to biblical multiplication

---

[6] 1–10 of the misconceptions related to evangelism, taken from the book *Evangelism Is . . . How to Share Christ with Passion and Confidence*, by Dave Earley & David Wheeler (Nashville: B&H, 2010), vii–ix.

among the church body. Biblical church planting is always born out of intentional evangelism. That was the model of the apostle Paul and the early church. According to Scripture, they first evangelized communities and then created congregations with the intention of training the new disciples to become reproducing Great Commission Worshippers. Biblical evangelism must always be the heartbeat of church planting!

Common Misconceptions of Worship

1. **Worship is when we come together at church on Sundays.** The problem here is that we have confused the idea of corporate worship with "doing" church rather than "being" the church. As mentioned earlier in this chapter, the heartbeat of worship is the daily response of obedience to the commands of Christ that result in our joining Him on mission. Unfortunately, if worship becomes something that only occurs at a specific time and location each week, we lose the holistic call to be worshippers as we journey through daily life. It is this type of thinking that produces the ridiculous commitment to a meeting place rather than to the person of Christ.

2. **Worshippers do not "do" evangelism.** The common misconception here is that worship somehow precludes any responsibility to evangelize, disciple new believers, or otherwise focus on other Christian disciplines. If worship is the fully obedient response to the commands of God for every believer, then every valid expression of worship should be done with the aim of multiplying the kingdom of God through evangelism. After all, Jesus came "to seek and to save that which was lost" (Luke 19:10 NKJV).

3. **Leading worship in public has little or no relationship to private worship.** This misconception can have a dangerous impact on the kingdom of God. It is the heartbeat of hypocrisy. What resides in the heart of man will ultimately reveal itself by way of a man's sinful actions and attitudes in daily life.

4. **Private worship and public (corporate) worship are essentially the same.** This concept builds off of the previous misconception. It

is a huge mistake to assume that you can substitute your times of private devotions with sporadic times of public worship. In the end, without regular times of private worship, one's public worship will become perverted and shallow. It is like building a house. Whereas public worship is like seeing the finished product, one's habits related to private worship are similar to the foundation being poured and the walls being framed.

5. **Worship is all about the music.** This is probably the greatest misconception as worship and music in the modern church have become synonymous. When someone says, "That was a great time of worship," it usually means that they enjoyed the time of singing and music. As mentioned earlier in reference to Abraham and Isaac, worship is about total obedience, *not* music. Unfortunately, it seems that "worship" is now synonymous with being entertained by talented musicians more than it is surrendering to a holy God!

6. **Worship does not include preaching.** Some believe worship only occurs when music is present. While music is an important aspect of worship in Scripture, it is the proclamation of God's Word that transforms people's lives and brings them to repentance. This is why the preacher and the person leading music need to work together in order to create a unified message for the worship service. If this is done correctly, then both the music and the message will serve to convict the worshippers and send them back to their mission fields recharged and ready to be become "fishers of men."

7. **Worshippers should focus more on building a relationship with God than on developing or nurturing relationships with people.** Again, this is a misconception that serves to draw worshippers away from impacting the world for Christ. Those who buy into this approach generally see themselves creating a "deeper life" with God that cannot be interrupted by anything—even taking the gospel to an unsaved friend or neighbor. While it is very important to build a deeper relationship with Christ through prayer and Bible study, if taken to the extreme it can become something akin to spiritual narcissism. The solution is to model the life of Christ, who always had time to build relationships with hurting people.

8. **There is no relationship between worship and obedience.** This misconception fosters the idea that one can worship without striving to live a holy life, and one's life does not impact the way he worships. As mentioned earlier, the heartbeat of worship is obedience to Christ and His commands. Without obedience worship may occur, but it will not be edifying in the biblical sense.

9. **Worship is primarily a young people's phenomenon.** This comes from the idea that worship and music are synonymous. Because younger believers are often more energetic and emotional in their responses, it can be easy to assume that worship is reserved for a younger crowd. Do not be fooled! Since worship is about obedience rather than emotional responses, the proof of real worship is found in the consistent lifestyle of individual believers regardless of their age.

10. **Worship is primarily based on my own personal experience.** The danger of this misconception is that it deifies one's preferences. The belief is, "If I don't have the right feeling, then I haven't worshipped." Nothing could be further from the truth. What if a person is convicted of sin during worship? That is usually not a positive experience. Are we to assume that real worship did not occur based on negative feelings? Absolutely not! Keep in mind that "real" worship will bring about "real" change, and that may not be "real" fun! Emotions are destined to change, while the truth always remains the same.

11. **Worship is a musical style.** Worship can often be minimized into a man-made box or particular style. We use terms like *blended*, *contemporary*, or even *traditional* worship. Worship is much more than the type of music that is played. In fact, worship is not a "service" to be attended. It is a surrendered approach to life that is to be lived out in all we do.

12. **Worship is a required task.** This misconception thinks of worship as a "task" on some to-do list that one is required to accomplish. But if worship is truly an act of obedience, it is much more than something to be merely checked off of a list. It is an expression of one's lifestyle that consistently reflects the character

of Christ. After all, He alone is the object of our worship. The only proper response is unhindered obedience.

Some Biblical Models

Now that we understand the basic connection between worship and evangelism, as well as a few misconceptions of each, it is time to examine some biblical models. Consider the following:

Romans 11:36–12:8 . . .

> For of Him and through Him and to Him are all things, to whom be glory forever. Amen. I beseech you therefore, brethren, by the mercies of God, that you present your bodies a living sacrifice, holy, acceptable to God, which is your reasonable service. And do not be conformed to this world, but be transformed by the renewing of your mind, that you may prove what is that good and acceptable and perfect will of God. For I say, through the grace given to me, to everyone who is among you, not to think of himself more highly than he ought to think, but to think soberly, as God has dealt to each one a measure of faith. For as we have many members in one body, but all the members do not have the same function, so we, being many, are one body in Christ, and individually members of one another. Having then gifts differing according to the grace that is given to us, let us use them: if prophecy, let us prophesy in proportion to our faith; or ministry, let us use it in our ministering; he who teaches, in teaching; he who exhorts, in exhortation; he who gives, with liberality; he who leads, with diligence; he who shows mercy, with cheerfulness. (Rom 11:36–12:8 NKJV)

Beginning with Rom 11:36, we are reminded that while "all things" belong to God, the ultimate *purpose* for His people is that He might receive "glory forever." This is why we live and worship: that God might be eternally exalted among the nations through the surrendered and obedient lives of His children.

It does not end here. We are implored to present our "bodies a living sacrifice, holy, acceptable to God, which *is* your reasonable service [worship]." In other words, our greatest act of worship is not merely responding to God as an act of blind compliance to a set of rules and standards. To the contrary, God requires that if His children are to be genuine worshippers, they must "be transformed by the renewing of your mind," in order to reveal to the unredeemed world the "good and acceptable and perfect will of God."

How is this to be accomplished in reference to evangelism and living out the Great Commission? First of all, biblical worship is never dormant, but should always drive the individual to unite with Christ in ministry. Real disciples are called to join Christ as He goes on mission to bring the world to Himself.

Therefore, after sacrificially worshipping God with a heart that is "transformed," the natural progression is to utilize one's gifts as an expression of worship in action. Note again how Paul explains our call:

> Having then gifts differing according to the grace that is given
> to us, let us use them: if prophecy, let us prophesy in proportion
> to our faith; or ministry, let us use it in our ministering; he who
> teaches, in teaching; he who exhorts, in exhortation; he who
> gives, with liberality; he who leads, with diligence; he who shows
> mercy, with cheerfulness. (Rom 12:6–8 NKJV)

Keep in mind that in this context the church is also referred to as being "one body." It should be traveling in the same direction with a common vision. As a result, while the gifts might differ in expression, they are the same in purpose: to glorify Christ in true worship that not only entices the soul to develop a deeper relationship with God but also electrifies the believer's heart to action that multiplies God's kingdom. In the end, this passage serves to balance the biblical concept of worship with the call of the Great Commission!

Matthew 22:36–40 . . .

> "Teacher, which is the great commandment in the law?" Jesus
> said to him, "'*You shall love the* LORD *your God with all your heart,*
> *with all your soul, and with all your mind.'* This is the first and
> great commandment. And the second is like it: *'You shall love*
> *your neighbor as yourself.'* On these two commandments hang all
> the Law and the Prophets." (Matt 22:36–40 NKJV)

This passage is affectionately known as *the Great Commandment*.
When Jesus was asked by the religious leaders "which *is* the great
commandment in the law?" he thoughtfully responded by first point-
ing them to the need of loving *"the* LORD *your God with all your heart,*
with all your soul, and with all your mind." He then expanded it to
include loving *"your neighbor as yourself."*

Within these brief and impactful words, we find the heart of both
worship and evangelism. There is the obvious call to glorify God with
unyielding allegiance, but it is not complete unless that message grows
beyond the immediate circle of self to include loving one's neighbor.

The assumption is that if an individual falls in love with Christ
and seeks to glorify His name, he or she will in turn express that same
love for people (neighbors) who invade their lives on a daily basis. In
addition, it must be noted that for either command to be fulfilled,
it is required that "self" must fall to the bottom of the list when it
comes to daily priorities. Worship, therefore, is not an impotent act
or staged event. Rather it is a passionate response to the heart cry of
God that includes active participation in the Great Commission.

John 12:23–26

As further evidence of this call to yield up one's life in service to
Christ and others, consider these words of Jesus:

> "The hour has come that the Son of Man should be glorified.
> Most assuredly, I say to you, unless a grain of wheat falls into the
> ground and dies, it remains alone; but if it dies, it produces much
> grain. He who loves his life will lose it, and he who hates his life

in this world will keep it for eternal life. If anyone serves Me, let him follow Me; and where I am, there My servant will be also. If anyone serves Me, him My Father will honor." (John 12:23–26 NKJV)

The bottom line is that true biblical worship requires a life that is totally sold out and obedient to the Master. In order for this concept to be complete, Christians have to be willing to die to self and to join Christ on mission every day. As Jesus states above, "If anyone serves Me, let him follow Me." Conversely, if you do not "follow" Him by adopting His passion in becoming "fishers of men," can you be called a true worshipper of God?

Beginning the Journey

As you can see from what has already been discussed, there is much confusion when it comes to clarifying the roles of worship and evangelism. All too often, well-meaning Christians attempt to separate the biblical concepts by defining them in the narrowest of terms.

Ultimately, the result has been a generation of misguided and anemic Christians who are clueless in reference to the idea of worship and how that concept translates into a lifestyle that multiplies the kingdom of God. The following chapters will build upon this dichotomy in order to restore the integrity of the Great Commission as a goal for discipling future generations of passionate believers.

With this in mind, you will want to pay special attention to the next chapter. It is based on Matt 28:16–20. Before the disciples receive from Jesus the Great Commission, they spend time in worship of Him as their risen Lord. It is only after they worship that He shares His credentials and gives them the power to do what they are called to do. It is only after they worship that they receive the promise of His presence as they accomplish what He has appointed them to do as ministers of the gospel.

Discussion Questions

1. How do worship and evangelism differ? How are they the same?

2. What is the purpose of the church? What is the purpose of individual believers?

3. How do you respond to the list of "What Evangelism Is Not"? Any surprises, additions, etc.?

4. How do you respond to the list of "What Worship Is Not"? Any surprises, additions, etc.?

5. What is the apparent connection between the Great Commission, the Great Commandment, the call to worship, and the call to evangelize (multiply)?

CHAPTER 2

Becoming a Great Commission Worshipper

The world can be saved by one thing and that is worship. For to worship is to quicken the conscience by the holiness of God, to feed the mind with the truth of God, to purge the imagination by the beauty of God, to open the heart to the love of God, to devote the will to the purpose of God.

William Temple[1]

It's been nearly 20 years since I first became a student of the Great Commission to worship. Robert Morgan, author of the hugely popular collection of hymn story books *Then Sings My Soul*, preached a sermon in which he showed that Jesus used the encounter in Matt 28:16–20 as an opportunity to demonstrate how the disciples worshipped before receiving the Great Commission. Later, I wrote a

---

[1] Quoted in Robert Morgan, ed., *Stories, Illustrations, and Quotes* (Nashville: Thomas Nelson, 2000), 808.

chapter in a book[2] where I showed the relationship between worship and the Great Commission. Since that time, my heart has turned to studying the connection between the two in greater detail.

Before going very far in developing the principles in Matthew 28 and unpacking the truth about worship and the Great Commission, it is important to gain perspective by answering five important questions. An understanding of the issues related to these questions will help establish parameters for the vast and dynamic subject of worship—especially as related to evangelism:

First, what is meant by the word *praise?* Often, when students are asked this question, they respond that praise is proclaiming the wonders of God or praise is magnifying the works of a sovereign God or praise is translating all of who God is into words simple enough for man to understand.

I usually respond by asking if there is a simpler way to state the definition. Some really bright student will almost always say, "Isn't praise just bragging on God?" Bingo! Praise is telling God how good He is. When we praise, we talk big about God. That's it. Nothing more. We tell God that we recognize His wonder, work, majesty, glory, and marvel—all of it.

God doesn't *need* for us to tell Him that He is good. He is fully aware of His attributes and qualities. No, we need to brag on God because when we do, we capture a vision of how big, awesome, wonderful, and good He is to us.

Offering praise to God is what we do in public and in private.

The second question is, "What is meant by the term *worship?*" Defining this word can become complicated. I've read commentaries that devote numerous pages to the idea that God is worthy of worship. One of the Old Testament words for worship is *shachah*—to kneel, stoop, prostrate oneself, or throw oneself down, in reverence.[3] The New Testament word for worship is *proskuneo.* This Greek term

---

[2] Vernon M. Whaley, *Understanding Music and Worship in the Local Church* (Wheaton, Il: Evangelical Training Association, 1995), 13–20.

[3] Vernon M. Whaley, *Called to Worship* (Nashville: Thomas Nelson, 2009), xv.

literally means kissing, bowing down, showing respect and adoration.[4] Charles Ryrie says that the English word "worship" is a shortened form of "worthship," meaning to attribute worth to the object worshipped.[5] *Unger's Bible Dictionary* defines *worship* as "the act of paying divine honors to a deity; religious reverence and homage."[6]

Obviously, our feeble attempt to define worship of the living Lord can go on and on. I've found that the simple and most accurate definition of worship is this: "Love God." Jesus said, "Love the LORD your God with all your heart, with all your soul, with all your mind, and with all your strength" (Mark 12:30 NKJV; cf. Matt 22:37; Luke 10:27). It is best evidenced when we personally tell the Lord that we love Him and Him alone. Our worship is then put into practice when we demonstrate our love by the way we live. We often call this *lifestyle worship*.

Our understanding of how, why, when, and where we worship is a clear reflection of the kind of relationship we have with God. It is a keenly personal experience. We often talk about how we gather together to worship the Lord. In reality, while we will sing songs, offer prayers, and preach in corporate settings, the actual act of worship of our God is keenly personal. It is a matter of the heart. Only God knows if one truly worships.

The third question to consider involves comparison between Old and New Testament worship. It is in the Old Testament that God establishes a covenant with Abraham in order to make a great nation and provide a pathway for all people to be redeemed from the penalty of sin and become worshippers of "the most high God."

In the Old Testament we find scores of biblical illustrations of men, women, boys, and girls offering worship to the Lord. The prophets preach about worship. The Patriarchs practice worship. The nations are blessed when they worship Yahweh.

---

[4] Ibid., xiv.

[5] Charles C. Ryrie, *Basic Theology: A Popular Systematic Guide to Understanding Biblical Truth* (Wheaton: Victor, 1988), 428.

[6] Merrill F. Unger, *Unger's Bible Dictionary* (Chicago: Moody, 1966), 1172.

In the Old Testament, God is careful to provide a method for worship. Remember, it is when Moses journeys to the top of Mount Sinai to receive from God the Ten Commandments that God gives instructions on how His chosen ones should worship. Old Testament believers sacrifice animals, provide grain offerings, and separate themselves from evil—all as demonstration of their obedience to God in worship of Him as the Lord, *Yahweh*. Old Testament worshippers seek forgiveness of sin through the intercession of a priest, the giving of tithes, and singing songs of praise.

In the Old Testament, we learn that God's desire is to "dwell with His people." From before the dawn of creation, God begins to establish a companionship with those that love Him. At first, God chooses to dwell in a box—the "ark of the covenant." Priests carry the "ark" every time the nomadic Jewish worshippers move from location to location and place to place. It is in the tabernacle or temple that God makes His presence known. People often travelled great distances to "find" God, receive forgiveness of sin, and seek His blessing.

In the New Testament, Jesus establishes a new covenant at the Last Supper (Matt 26:17–30; Mark 14:12–26; Luke 22:7–20). With Jesus' death, burial, and resurrection, God chooses to provide a "more perfect way" for us to worship (Heb 9:1–15).

In the Old Testament, God chooses to dwell in the tabernacle and temple. In the New Testament, He chooses to dwell in the hearts of man and woman. He is God in us.

The Old Testament covenant had regulations for worship in the tabernacle or temple. These meeting places had a lamp stand, table, consecrated bread, and a holy place. Behind a second curtain was a room called the Most Holy Place. In the Most Holy Place was the golden altar of incense and gold-covered ark of the covenant. This ark contained the gold jar of manna, Aaron's staff that budded, and the stone tablets of the covenant—the Ten Commandments. The priests entered the outer room regularly to carry on their ministry. But only the high priest entered the Most Holy Place once each year to offer sacrifices for the sins of the world.

Even though the sins of the people were atoned for during these times, the "gifts and sacrifices being offered were not able to clear the conscience of the worshipper" (Heb 9:9–10 NIV).

In New Testament times, the old regulations were abandoned and God chose to dwell in the hearts of His children. The role of the priest was forever changed. When Christ died on the cross and rose victorious from the grave, He became our high priest. He entered the Most Holy Place once for all by His own blood. Jesus is able to *cleanse our consciences* (Heb 9:14) from acts of sin. Christ Jesus stands today as the mediator of this new covenant so that many may receive eternal life. Jesus stands today as our high priest. Why? So that we will become worshippers.

The fourth question centers on the focus and purpose of the New Testament: "What is the main focus of New Testament worship?" One simple word—Jesus. Everything relating to worship in the Old Testament—the tabernacle, temple, sacrifices—all point to Jesus. When we arrive in the New Testament, we find that *everything* is complete in Jesus. It is this one principle that makes the "new covenant" introduced by Jesus at the Last Supper so significant. The new covenant is what gives Jesus reason to say, "I am the way, the truth, and the life."

What makes Jesus so important to worship is that He alone provides our way to God. He is our advocate, our justification, our righteousness, our high priest, and our worship leader. It is only because of Jesus' death on the cross and resurrection from the dead that we can enter boldly into the throne of Grace. *All* of the Old Testament symbols, laws, rituals, and regulations point to God's ultimate plan—Jesus. God fulfilled His desire of being *God with Us* through the work of His son.

The final question involves specific practices of worship: "What are the guiding principles used by the disciples and early Christians to establish a scriptural pattern or model for worship?" Historical record gives little indication of worship structure for the early Christians. There are few "orders of worship." Much of their early practice parallels Jewish practice with emphasis on dates, seasons, and special emphases. They met in synagogues and later in mixed gatherings of Jews and Gentiles.

As the early Christians were scattered to other nations because of persecution and fear of death, the structure of their services became less and less important. As a result, Jesus, not ritual, underscored the focus of early New Testament worship—Jesus as the totally divine, physical representation of the invisible God. Weekly Sabbath meetings, often held in the synagogue, centered on the teachings of Jesus. Weekly gatherings for fellowship and celebration of the Lord's Supper focused on Jesus. Healings were in Jesus' name. In general, two basic emphases emerge in the daily life of the early Christians: personal worship of Jesus and fulfillment of the Great Commission.

In Matt 28:1–10 and 16–20, Jesus provides a model for becoming Great Commission worshippers. A Great Commission worshipper is a person who is so much in love with Jesus, so committed to worship of Jesus, and so devoted to being obedient to every command of Jesus that he simply cannot restrain himself from telling others about his incredible relationship with the Son of God. A Great Commission Worshipper is equally committed to worship and evangelism. There is never a time when a division is made between the two. This concept of worship-evangelism is the biblical model for discipleship. It is not a new paradigm for evangelism. For us in the twenty-first century, however, it is a model that needs to be articulated again and again. As our understanding of this model unfolds before our eyes, we learn that in the process a Christian can become a Great Commission worshipper of the only true God.

Let's look first at the setting of Matthew 28. This is the well-known passage where "Mary, and the other Mary" discover Jesus is victorious over death. He has been raised from the dead. It is the day after the Sabbath—Sunday morning. When the women get to the empty tomb, the angel makes the announcement: "He is not here. He has risen from the dead as he said he would. Come and see the place where his body was" (Matt 28:6 NCV). The angel tells the women to quickly return and tell his followers that Jesus has risen and is going ahead of them into Galilee (Matt 28:7). The women immediately obey. As they leave the tomb, Jesus reveals Himself to the women. They immediately fall down on their faces, clasp Jesus' feet, and worship Him. Jesus tells them, "Don't be afraid. Go and tell my followers to go on to Galilee, and they will see me there" (Matt 28:9–10 NCV). Again, they immediately obey.

The scene then turns to Galilee and the planned meeting Jesus has called with His disciples. "The eleven followers went to Galilee to the mountain where Jesus had told them to go" (Matt 28:16 NCV). First, Jesus calls for a meeting. This is the same Jesus whom everyone, including the disciples, thought was dead. Second, it is a very special meeting. Apparently, only the disciples are invited. The Bible does not give any record of any other people being invited to this time with Jesus. Third, this is a significant meeting. It is the first time all eleven disciples have been together with Jesus since the Last Supper. Fourth, at this meeting, Jesus reveals His strategy for the disciples to carry on the work of the ministry. Jesus' plan is to lay on their hearts the mission, ministry, passion, and dynamic of the Great Commission.

Fifth, this is the first of many meetings before He returns to His Father in heaven (Acts 1:7–10). I'm certain that with each encounter Jesus took time to share strategic plans and ideas about how the kingdom of God could and should be advanced. Jesus desires to spend time with His disciples. He loves them. They love Him. In the transition, He gives them a lesson regarding how to be Great Commission Worshippers.

The Pattern for Worship (Matt 28:16a)

The disciples *get away from the busyness of life in order* to be with Jesus. *"Then the eleven disciples went away into Galilee"* (Matt 28:16a NKJV). Obviously, the disciples were not distracted by cell phones, e-mail, television, Twitter, or Facebook as we are. I'm certain they were often sidetracked by the clamor of a daily routine and the draw of immediate (often unimportant) commotions, interruptions, diversions, and confusion of the normal work day.

Jesus wanted their undivided attention. He wanted them to get away from the distractions, the work, and other outside influences. Why? So that they could focus on Jesus. Our Lord knew the disciples would be tempted to do other things and not devote themselves to Him and Him alone. So, they went away.

Just like those disciples, we need to get away from the busyness of life in order to be with Jesus. He wants us to block out time during the course of our busy day for the sole purpose of being alone with our Lord. Just as He desired to be with those disciples centuries ago, He wants to spend time with us today.

Unlike the disciples, we *are* distracted by a fast-paced information culture that constantly seeks to capture our social, moral, intellectual, and spiritual concentration and energies. We are bombarded by 24-hour cable news and information, an ever-invasive addiction to social networking, a carnal postmodern secular culture, and the temptation to fill our egos with the temporal, self-indulgent arrogance of this age.

Think about it. How many times have you and I sat down to spend a few precious minutes with the Lord only to be distracted by the "quick check" of an e-mail? By the time we've finished wording our e-mail, the moments set aside for reading God's Word and breathing a few precious words in prayer are gone. We are taking care of the urgent, but ignore that which will nurture our eternal soul.

If we are going to become successful Great Commission Worshippers, we need to get away from the busy times and places of life.

The Place for Worship (Matt 28:16b)

The second principle in becoming a Great Commission Worshipper involves going to an appointed place. *"The eleven disciples went away into Galilee, to the mountain which Jesus had appointed for them"* (Matt 28:16b NKJV). Just as it is critical that we get away from the frantic pace of life and meet with Jesus, it is equally important that we go to a special, designated location for that meeting—an appointed place.

It really doesn't matter what place is designated for the meeting. All of us need to get away and go to a place where we can be alone with Jesus. Sometimes that place may be the solitude of a car on the way to work. Sometimes it may be that the meeting with Jesus is alone in a bathroom or closet. The time of day is unimportant. Many people meet with God early in the morning before the hurry and confusion of the day set in. Others enjoy meeting God late at night.

This special location needs to be a place to which one can return time and time again. Some people like to go to a special place in the woods—surrounded by the beauty of nature. Others like to go to the top of a mountain. It really doesn't matter where one goes to be alone with the Lord. What is important in becoming a worshipper is that a special place has been established for a regular meeting with God that is easily accessible to the regular routine of life.

During the early part of my junior year in college, my friend Jonathan Thigpen stopped me and asked if I wanted to go to the storage closet and pray. It was a Monday. I was walking from my room to the bathroom in our college dormitory when Jonathan asked me if I wanted to join him in prayer. I reluctantly agreed. We walked into the large storage closet on the second floor of Goen Hall. Over in the far left-hand corner, Jonathan had built a makeshift desk. He used an old motel suitcase stand as the main platform, folded some beach towels over the top, and placed a lamp on the far right-hand corner of the surface. His Bible and some writing materials were lying on the towels. I asked about a chair. He said, "Well, I usually just kneel, but on occasion I use one of these suitcases,"

"What do you do?" I asked.

Jonathan carefully explained that he came to this storage closet every night at 9:30 just to meet with God. He told me that he usually read a passage of Scripture, made a list of his prayer items on the pad in front of him, and then began to pray.

We read Colossians, chapter one. I wrote down a couple of "things" I thought were important: great classes the next week, safety for our quartet and our travels on the weekend, and discipline as we entered into the new school year. I looked over at Jonathan's list. It was long and beside each item was a date. I asked Jonathan, "What's the date for?" "Oh, I write down the date on which I make the request to the Lord and the day when God answers my prayer," he replied.

After a few moments, I bowed my head and took my wish list to the Lord: Bless mom and dad, sister and brother—all in North Carolina; bless the new school year; bless the quartet as we travel for the college; bless our teachers; and, bless the missionary families overseas. To me, it felt like I had prayed for hours. Nope. Three minutes. I'm not sure I remember how long Jonathan prayed, but it must have been quite a while because he got through his entire list.

The two of us began meeting on a regular basis to pray in that storage room. At first it was two times each week. Later, we met four and five times each week. For more than a full year, the two of us met in that storage room for the singular purpose of spending time with Jesus.

We prayed for friends, neighbors, fellow students, and family. Mostly, we prayed to God about our own need to know the Lord on a more personal, dynamic basis. We asked God to show us His plan for our lives. He did. I remember us asking God to teach us to pray. He did. Over that next year God answered hundreds of prayers—big and small. We faithfully recorded the dates of those answered prayers in our notebooks. My brother received Jesus Christ in his heart as a result of our prayer times together. As a result of those times alone with God—at an appointed place—the two of us formed a two-man evangelistic team and traveled all across the country, preaching and singing. Hundreds of young people received Christ during those meetings. We participated in scores of all-night prayer meetings. In the process, we began to value that special place where we enjoyed time alone with God.

The Person of Worship (Matt 28:17a)

Becoming a Great Commission Worshipper involves seeing Jesus. "*On the mountain they saw Jesus*" (Matt 28:17a). They recognized Jesus. This is the same Jesus whom the disciples thought was dead—forever out of their lives. This same Jesus is now walking across that mountain path, coming toward them. Can you imagine the sheer emotion of the moment? This was Jesus—Son of Man, Son of God, friend, companion, rabbi, and Lord. This was the same Jesus, but *this* Jesus was different.

It is the same Jesus who healed the sick. It is the same Jesus who raised the lifeless bodies from the clutches of death. It is the same Jesus who ran the moneychangers out of the temple, but this Jesus is different.

Yes, it *is* the same Jesus who said, "Suffer little children to come unto me, and forbid them not: for of such is the kingdom of God" (Luke 18:16 KJV; see also Matt 19:14; Mark 10:14). It *is* the same Jesus who calmed the sea, fed the thousands, and spoke "peace, be still," but, *this* Jesus is different.

How is *this* Jesus different? This is the resurrected Jesus. This Jesus is victorious over death and the grave. This Jesus makes it possible for you and me to worship the Lord of the universe, to have eternal life. Yes, it *is* the same Jesus who performed all the miracles, but this time, Jesus comes to the disciples as redeemer, savior, all-forgiving, all-loving, ever-faithful Lord of lords and King of kings. The disciples saw *this* Jesus. They recognized Him with both their physical and spiritual eyes.

In order to become a Great Commission Worshipper, we must see and recognize Jesus for who He really is. He is much more than a prophet, miracle maker, peace-giver, rabbi, and all-around good guy. No. This is the Christ, the Son of the living God. This Jesus is the one and only person in the universe who is 100 percent God and 100 percent man—all the time. It is *this* Jesus whom you and I must see—recognize, comprehend, distinguish, identify, grasp, understand, know, and follow before we can hope to become Great Commission Worshippers.

What happens when we really see and recognize Jesus?

The Process (Matt 28:17b)

We worship! It is when we fully see and understand Jesus as Lord of lords, King of kings, our righteous and sovereign God that we fall down and worship. We literally cannot help it. Worship is the natural response to God's revelation. The Bible indicates that *"when they saw Him, they worshiped Him"* (Matt 28:17b NKJV). Down through the ages, anytime a person encounters the living God, the immediate result is worship—usually facedown worship.

Abraham encountered God after battle, paid tithes, and worshipped. Jacob wrestled with God during the night and worshipped—he named the place Bethel. Moses worshipped after meeting God in the burning bush. Joshua met the *Captain of the King's Army* and worshipped. Solomon worshipped after God consumed the sacrifice with fire. Isaiah saw the Lord, worshipped, and confessed. Elijah witnessed the fire of God, worshipped God, and defeated the prophets of Baal.

In the first part of this passage, Matt 28:1–10, as Mary leaves to go and tell the disciples that Jesus is alive, "Behold, Jesus met them, saying, "Rejoice!" So they came and held Him by the feet and worshiped Him" (Matt 28:9–10 NKJV). Mary's immediate reaction to hearing Jesus' voice is to fall down on her face, grab His feet and worship.

The list can go on and on. Remember, every time God reveals Himself to mankind, the immediate and most forthright result is worship. Why should it be any different here? The disciples see Jesus, and their first reaction is to worship.

Do you remember our definition of worship in the beginning of this chapter? In short, worship is to love God. I'm confident those disciples did just that—love on Jesus. Perhaps they surrendered to Him, showed their deep affection to Him by hugging His neck. Perhaps they fell to their knees or jumped up and down. We don't know. When they saw Jesus, however, their immediate response was to worship.

When we see Jesus, we will worship. We will show our love *to Him* individually. No one can love Jesus for us. Remember, worship is a deeply personal relationship between you and God.

We will need to exhibit our love *for Him* in the way we live day by day. Our love for Him is often demonstrated in the way we treat other people, react to large and small crises throughout the day, and respond to the challenge of the "must get ahead" culture around us. We need to aggressively make obvious our love *of Him* to the dying world around us. Simply put: our worship of Him will compel us to share with those around us the wonders of God.

Perhaps we too can capture a sense of the awesome victory the disciples felt in their hearts when they saw Jesus. They worshipped because they were in the presence of Jesus—totally abandoned to worship of Him as the Risen Lord. We can do the same. We can worship Jesus—totally abandoned from the distractions of this world and focused on the person, work, and wonder of Jesus.

The Problems (Matt 28:17c)

The Bible doesn't make clear just who is at this meeting with Jesus. Certainly one can assume that Peter, James, and John were there, but that leaves eight of the remaining eleven disciples in question. Remember, Judas was no longer with them, and they had not elected Matthias as his replacement.

The next part of this lesson from Jesus always puzzles me. "Some doubted" (Matt 28:17c NKJV). Some doubted? Yes, right in the middle of the celebration and worship are those who doubt this is really Jesus. Others doubt the worship is genuine. I'm sure some doubt because they think the public display of worship is too emotional.

Would you like to know what I would have done if those doubters had been in my worship service? I am so certain that after the first complaint I would have said something like this: "Hey, you doubters, get out of here. We don't need your spirit of negativity around here." I would have done everything in my power to purge that meeting from those that did not truly believe. In my heart of hearts, I would have justified the loss. That is not what Jesus did.

He did not chase them away. He didn't tell them to go to some other meeting down the street. Not Jesus. Rather, He ministered to the doubter and the believer alike.

He met their needs. He did not isolate them. He did not chide them. He did not rebuke them. He loved them and ministered as if they fully believed.

Isn't that just like Jesus? He sought to minister to everyone who came to that meeting at the point of their deepest need.

There will always be doubters. Always! There will always be those who say what God is doing is not of God. It has been that way with every revival recorded in church history.

Some will say, "It is too emotional." Others, "It is not intellectual enough."

Some will look you right in the eye and accuse you of being out of the will of God. They will judge your music. They will judge your method of evangelism. They will judge your motives. That is what doubters do. What should you do in response? You hold your head up high and minister to the doubter and believer alike. Why?

You can count on it. There will be a time when that doubter will need you. It may be in the middle of the night that you receive a phone call. On the other end of the line is that doubter. This time the death angel has visited the doubter's home. The oldest son or daughter of that family has been killed. You get out of bed, hurry to the hospital, and meet the family. You might hear that the doubter has been taken by some strange disease. In response, you minister peace, hope, and love to the doubter. Why? Jesus ministered to the doubter. When you minister to the doubter in love, it is not long until they become believers, too.

The Power for Worship (Matt 28:18)

Down through the centuries, God has always responded to those who genuinely worship Him. Always. This time, He responds by telling the disciples something critically important about Himself. *"All power is given unto me,"* He declares (Matt 28:18 KJV). This is

His credential. It is His proof of ability or trustworthiness. It is the authentic evidence and confirmation that Jesus is the "real deal."

I teach at a university. Almost everyone who studies here is working toward the completion of the baccalaureate, master's, or doctoral degree. In all my years, I have yet to see a time at graduation when even one student walks across the platform, shakes hands with the provost or president of the institution, and says, "No thanks, I know I've finished all the work, paid all the money, and done every assignment needed to receive this award, but let someone else have my diploma." Why? The degree—the parchment—the paper itself—represents completed work. It is the credential. Every student working toward an advanced degree is looking to receive the documentation that "shows the world" he or she is qualified to do something. The credential confirms a person's position or status. In some cases, a person cannot obtain gainful employment without the credential. Teachers must have a degree with licensure in order to receive state certification. Lawyers must have the *Juris Doctorate Degree (J.D.)* in order to take the bar exam. Physicians must have received the *Doctor of Medicine (M.D.)* so that they may take the appropriate medical exams. Credentials are essential to success in our fast-paced, intellectually driven culture.

Remember, the Jesus standing before these disciples is different from the Jesus they knew before the crucifixion. Jesus tells the disciples that He is the recipient of *all power.* What He means by the term *all* is that He encompasses *all of the power of heaven and earth.* Jesus makes the claim that He is omnipotent. There is no greater power, and this power is from God, *given* exclusively to Jesus.

It would be enough if the descriptive of this power ended with this declaration. But there is much more. This power is personally given by God Himself and received by the Son. While I don't pretend to know all the theological implications of that one statement, I do know this power has authority. It is active. It is a living, vibrant power. Jesus is giving His power to those disciples, and He wants to give that power to us as well.

It is His power that transforms lives and sets captives free. It is through the power of Jesus that cultures are radically renovated and political darkness halted.

It is through the power of Jesus that the world can know the forgiveness of sin.

Jesus has the power to alter totally the course of history. Jesus gives this power to a group of faithful worshippers. Through their efforts they literally change the world for the kingdom of God.

The Presence in Worship (Matt 28:19–20a)

Now, we come to the passage of Scripture that missiologists and teachers of evangelism often use—the Great Commission. Jesus says, "Go therefore and make disciples of all the nations, baptizing them in the name of the Father and of the Son and of the Holy Spirit, teaching them to observe all things that I have commanded you" (Matt 28:19–20a NKJV). The command to go is direct. The command to make disciples is decisive. The command to baptize in the name of the Father, Son, and Holy Spirit is defined. The command to observe all things is definite. With this command is the promise of the ages: "Lo, I am with you always, *even* to the end of the age." Jesus gives these disciples His presence.

His presence will be with them at all times. His presence will go with them everywhere. His presence will be sufficient for every task (teaching, baptizing, making disciples). His presence will be everlasting—even to the end of the age.

In direct response to the disciples' worship (Matt 28:16–17), Jesus provides His power and presence (vv. 18–20).

Summary: Principles for Great Commission Worship

How does one become a Great Commission Worshipper?

First, practice the principle of getting away from the busyness of life. Turn off the cell phone. Shut down the e-mail. Close the door.

Go someplace where you are not distracted by the things of this busy world.

Second, go to an appointed place where you and God can meet on a regular basis—alone.

Third, recognize Jesus as the risen, sovereign Lord.

Fourth, spend quality time worshipping Jesus. He is Lord. He is King of kings. He alone is the savior of the world. He is our worship leader.

Fifth, worship even when there are those around who doubt. There will be doubters—count on it.

Sixth, receive or accept His power upon your life and ministry. His power saves people from sin. Through His power we find success.

Seven, receive His presence as you go into all the world. God will honor you as He fills you with the indwelling presence of the Holy Spirit. It is the Spirit of God working in your life that allows you and me to become Great Commission Worshippers.

In our next chapter, we will discover how God equips us for Great Commission worship. We will investigate a strategy for preparation that establishes a worship model for ministry that is applicable to any culture, ethnic group, denominational group, or demographic.

Discussion Questions

1. Explain the term *lifestyle worship*. Give some biblical examples.

2. Discuss worship in the Old and New Testaments. How was it the same? How did it differ?

3. Fully discuss the biblical "pattern for worship." How does the principle impact your personal life of worship?

4. Fully discuss the "place of worship." Where do you worship?

5. Obviously, Jesus is the "Person" of worship. How does "process of worship" impact your life? Discuss any "problems" related to worship.

CHAPTER 3

Living a New Model for Worship

Jesus was born of a virgin, suffered under Pontius Pilate, died on the cross, and rose from the grave to make worshippers out of rebels.

A. W. Tozer[1]

We live in an incredible moment of church history. Thousands of churches today seek qualified worship leaders. These practitioners of worship and music are assuming roles in ministry that were only given to senior pastors ten or twenty years ago. Our twenty-first-century worship leaders teach biblical theology just as much as they teach music. Often, they are in the position to shape a congregation's concept of God, Christian service, evangelism, Christian graces, and discipleship—all through worship. They stand beside and join with their senior pastor (who is the chief worship leader for a congregation) in proclaiming the name of Jesus, imparting truth, engaging and activating the fellowship, and providing ministry to God and His people. Never in the history of the evangelical church has the worship

---

[1] A. W. Tozer, *What Ever Happened to Worship?* (Camp Hill, PA: Christian Publications, 1895), 9–10.

leader been given this kind of important role in ministry. God is ush-
ering in one of the greatest moments of spiritual awakening ever in
the history of the church.

It is my opinion that God, in His sovereignty, has chosen *this*
generation as recipients of another *Great Awakening*. Most historians
and worship theologians will agree that today's twenty-first-century
church is in the midst of a great worship awakening. In the process,
we are experiencing a paradigm shift in *the way* the evangelical
church worships.

God is providing opportunity to communicate the gospel in ways
only dreamed about even a decade ago. Information about almost any
subject is practically available at our fingertips. Well over half of the
American public access the Internet from their homes. We sit in our
living rooms watching 24-hour news programs and complete research
in seconds through Google that once required weeks of hard, focused,
on-the-ground investigative inquiry. Social networking is a way of
life. Facebook and YouTube provide pathways for communication
that can make unknown artists a success almost overnight. Social
networking can destroy a politician's career in moments and create
the "buzz" needed for building new, dynamic communities of faith.
Dating, courtship, and marriage are often accomplished on line. Social
media also provide a safe, albeit not necessarily healthy, place to hide
from the cares and realities of life.

These communication methods provide for the worship leader
a host of opportunities for teaching and leading worship. More
and more evangelical churches are hiring full-time worship leaders
skilled in multiple areas of technology. Music at some multisite
church services is sometimes coordinated for simultaneous music
presentation through fiber-optic communication. Scores of pastors
provide sermon illustrations and interview missionaries on the field
live from their pulpits on Sunday morning via i-chat, Skype, live-
Web streaming, or Go-to-Meeting.com. Literally scores of dot-com
companies eagerly await the opportunity to provide the twenty-first-
century worship leader with video clips, music, graphics, and Web
site resources—all for facilitating worship.

Likewise, many of the changes taking place for worship are mirrored by paradigm shifts and methodological nuances for church staffing, evangelism, children and student worship, church training, discipleship, and church administration. In short, we just don't "do" church like we used to do it.

Today's twenty-first-century church is a product of change. Worship in the church reflects dynamic change in culture, popular music, education, and the even the economy. The church has always adjusted to these changes in culture, various methods of communications, political uncertainties, war, educational challenges, and even natural disasters. Brace yourself. More change is coming.

Just a few years ago church strategists were talking about reaching the Boomers, Busters, and Generation X. Then, the Millennials and the Nexers. In a few years, another generation will come, and church strategists and missiologists will find yet a different label for identifying the needs of this next group.

As we face the reality of change and consider the most efficient and effective way to reach out to the passing generations in love, share Christ, preach the gospel, teach worship, and utilize innovative methodology, it is essential we focus on that which helps keep personal and professional perspective. It is important that we construct and establish a blueprint—a model, if you will—for Great Commission worship that will serve as an archetype for ministry during the uncertainty of change. This model needs to be broad in application so that it may apply to every ministry paradigm, especially evangelism and worship. The model also needs to be specific so that it measures up to the rigors of biblical truth, every time.

Before we investigate this blueprint—and certainly before we make application of the model to evangelism and worship—let's articulate at least four of the major influences that shape the way each of us perceives biblical mandates.

Major Influences

Our Calling

God has placed in each of us a *call to ministry*. It is *the calling* that gives focus, direction, and purpose. Often our decisions about ministry, relationships, and life careers are based on the perception we have about calling. Ephesians 4:1–3 (NIV) encourages us to *"live a life worthy of the calling"* by being humble, gentle, patient, and bearing with one another in love. The apostle Peter exhorts the believers to *"confirm [the] calling and election"* (2 Pet 1:10 NIV). The apostle Paul, in praying for the brothers and sisters in Thessalonica, asked God to *make [them] worthy of his calling, and . . . bring to fruition . . . every desire for goodness"* (2 Thess 1:11 NIV).

In the life of each believer, there are actually two kinds of callings: general and individual. The *general callings* include issues like salvation, obedience, faithfulness, evangelism, worship, and holiness. This is actually the intent of Peter's admonishment when he encourages believers to *confirm their calling and election*. All are called to salvation. All of us are *called* to be obedient, holy, righteous, and faithful.

There is also the *individual calling* each of us receives. Every believer receives a unique calling that serves something like a compass when making decisions and discovering new and innovative ways to serve the Lord. *Individual calling* often becomes the determining factor in where we serve, what career and field we choose for lifetime ministry, and the vocation we choose to follow. This calling is deeply personal.

It is because this *calling* is deeply personal that we are prone to react when someone suggests that as we get older we should consider alternative venues for ministry. As we examine the need, implication, and scope of this model for worship and evangelism, we will begin to see that its application in our own lives is greatly influenced by our *individual callings*.

Our Experiences

All of us are products of our own life experiences. We bring to the ministry the good and bad of our own life encounters. Every experience—event, happening, perception, orientation, and context in life—shapes us at one level or another. As a result, all of us view life, ministry, service, giftedness, and, to a great extent, *calling*, as we are influenced by our own life experiences.

My mother and father were missionaries to Alaska. I grew up seeing life through the lens of a full-time pastor/missionary father. My parents were extraordinary in their expressions of love for me. They were encouragers and champions for many of my successes in life. For that matter, other people were recipients of my parents' generous love, affection, and encouragement. I am a product of their care and love for me today.

Likewise, everything we did as a family related in one way or another to my dad's own life experiences. He grew up on a farm in eastern North Carolina. His father was a share-cropper farmer. His great grandfather was a farmer who left the fields to fight in the Confederate Army.

Everything my dad did, even as an aging senior citizen, was a reflection of his own life experiences. He grew up during the dark days of the Great Depression, worked as a farmer until September 1940 when he enlisted in the army. He answered the call to the gospel ministry the night before shipping out for the New Hebrides Islands in the South Pacific during the uncertain days of World War II. Because of my dad's early experience on the farm, he was rarely interested in football, baseball, or most any group sports. Consequently, my dad's early life experience had significant impact on my life, too.

One of my best friends, on the other hand, grew up in the home of an alcoholic. His dad was sometimes physically and mentally abusive. His mother was understandably withdrawn and insecure. As a child, there were times when my friend felt unloved, alone, and unwanted. He rarely received encouragement from his mother and father. Our family loved him dearly, reached out to him on many occasions, had him in our home for days at a time, and sought to encourage him as a brother in the Lord. Even so, as an adult, he fell victim to the same kinds of lifestyle decisions that haunted his dad. By the age of 20, my childhood friend was a confirmed alcoholic. Obviously, he was deeply influenced by his life experiences.

In reality, our life experiences, good and bad, influence the way we view God's plan for us, His call on our lives, and the way we relate to others. It has always been that way. So, when we consider the model for evangelism and worship, most of us will also view its application through the prism of our own life experience.

Our Education

Closely related to the principle of life experience is education. All of us are in one way or another products of our educational experiences—both formal and informal. Mentor and long-time record producer Bob MacKenzie always said to aspiring music producers, arrangers, artists, publishers, and industry specialists, *"The longer the line of preparation, the greater the opportunity."*

Simply put, the longer we work at perfecting our calling, improving our gifts, and crafting our skills, the better the chance God will open greater doors of opportunity and influence. Mr. MacKenzie was right. God uses our educational experiences to prepare us for kingdom work. Our life experiences along with the education encounters help equip us for various opportunities in life.

Many times the days of preparation are difficult and grueling. The Old Testament patriarch Joshua spent 40 years in the land of Egypt under the oppressive rule of Pharaoh. There he learned how to be submissive, respect authority, and trust in the hand of God to provide, guide, and deliver him from evil. Joshua spent the next 40 years in an apprenticeship with Moses. Under Moses' leadership Joshua learned how to develop a friendship with God, avoid the perils of idol worship, trust the Lord to part the waters of the Red Sea, provide manna in the wilderness, and defeat the enemies of the Lord. Finally, at age 80, Joshua served in the position as "leader of the people of God." Even then, he only kept that position for 25 years.

In one true sense, those of us given the task and responsibility of leading God's people need to remain always students. We need to take every opportunity to be learners. What we do with the moments, circumstances, and events that come our way often makes the difference in our life successes many years later.

Our Opportunities

The final area of influence that impacts the way we view worship and evangelism involves opportunity. The word *opportunity* has already been used to define our experiences and educational background. Here, we are talking about *opportunity* as a noun. There are two types of opportunity. The idea of an opportunity may refer to someone getting *their big break* or *job opening*. Sometimes, this kind of opportunity is when a person has *occasion* to excel or gets a *chance* to prove themselves and their abilities for a specific task or assignment. Opportunity also refers to that which we encounter in our everyday walk in life. Sometimes God gives opportunity for us to talk with the person next to us on the airplane, standing in the line at the grocery store, or using the pump next to us at the gas station. At other times, God opens doors of opportunity for us to serve on the mission field, at the local rescue mission, as part of an evangelism team, with a new church plant, or as worship leader for a youth camp.

The point here is that we are products of our opportunities—great and small—good and bad. Our view of God, His work in our lives, His commitment to use us, and even the responsibility we have for worship and evangelism are to a great extent based on how well we manage the life opportunities that come our way.

God wants us to take the opportunity to know, love, and work unselfishly for Him. He desires that we live in such a way that we share the wonders of His person, presence, power, peace, and promise. He wants us to take every opportunity to reach out to those who are hurting and share His physical, spiritual, and emotional power to heal. He wants us to share the good news and tell the world that God is good, and He wants every man, woman, boy, and girl to become worshippers of Him as the Most High God.

The Worship Outcomes

Often when creating a new course or program of study, the person designing the curriculum or degree develops a series of *program learning outcomes (PLOs)*. Learning outcomes are what students are expected to demonstrate upon completion of a program, course, or activity. Often, the course designer will use action verbs and simple language to make the outcomes measurable and meaningful to the student's experience. For those of us in higher education, the phrase "program learning outcomes" brings to mind an important part of the teaching and training process. The whole idea when establishing clearly articulated PLOs is to facilitate for students the connections between classroom learning and real-life experiences.

In one true sense, our blueprint for Great Commission worship may serve as a set of outcomes that help us stay focused on our calling—worship evangelism. This model thus serves as a guideline for what all Great Commission worship should accomplish in the hearts of believers. That is because Great Commission worship is *formational, transformational, relational, missional, and reproducible.*

In the following chapters, we will unpack each one of these outcomes individually. But first, let's articulate a general overview of each:

1. Great Commission worship is **formational**. If the worship we do and the evangelism we give ourselves to is biblical, it should sculpt, form, and shape us. That's because we are shaped by our understanding of Scripture, comprehension of theology, and application of Christian doctrine. The Holy Spirit takes our own dynamic walk with Christ and uses it as opportunity to mold, fashion, and shape us into His image. This happens just a little bit every time we feast on the Word of God, worship the God of the Word, understand more fully the application of His Word on our lives, share the gospel with a friend, and experience His mercies new every morning. *Our worship of God*

and the evangelism we engage in is formational. (See diagram 1 on page 53.)

2. Great Commission worship is **transformational**. God is in the process of changing us from old to new. In writing to the believers in Rome, the apostle Paul said that we are not to *"be conformed to this world, but be transformed by the renewing of [our] mind, that [we] may prove what is that good and acceptable and perfect will of God"* (Rom 12:2 NKJV).

God is in the transformation business. He changes people. He uses agents like you and me to get that job done. We teach, train, encourage, edify, and share the gospel with the lost for the sole purpose of seeing God do His work in the lives of men and women, boys and girls. The Holy Spirit transforms lives from dead to living or hurting and broken to healed and restored. In this process, God takes a broken person and transforms them into a worshipper of the Most High God. *Great Commission worship is transformational.* (See diagram 1on page 53.)

3. Great Commission worship is **relational**. Our worship and the mandate for a biblical answer to evangelism are driven by our relationship to God and others. The dynamic between these two types of relationship enables us to understand the purpose for evangelism, the partnership between worship and evangelism, and our motive for evangelism and worship.

God is all about relationships. God desires to *be with us.* And He desires a relationship with you and me.

Our relationship with God should enable us to build, shape, develop, and cultivate a relationship with those around us. Again, the apostle Paul puts this in perspective:

> For I say, through the grace given to me, to everyone who is
> among you, not to think of himself more highly than he ought
> to think, but to think soberly, as God has dealt to each one a
> measure of faith. For as we have many members in one body,
> but all the members do not have the same function, so we, being
> many, are one body in Christ, and individually members of one
> another. . . . Rejoice with those who rejoice, and weep with those

who weep. Be of the same mind toward one another. Do not set your mind on high things, but associate with the humble. Do not be wise in your own opinion. (Rom 12:3–5,15–16 NKJV)

When God has called us home to glory, people will remember more about the relationship we had with them than the money in our pocket or credit card in our hands. They will remember if we were kind, gracious, loving, and accepting. They will remember us for who we are, what we represent, and how well we treat them. *Great Commission worship is relational.* (See diagram 1 on page 53.)

4. Great Commission Worship is ***missional****.* *Formational, transformational,* and *missional* are "hot words" in our emerging-church, post-modern culture. Their intent and application to our own daily living reach far past the novelty and triteness of language. Their use helps form and shape vision, focus, direction, and provide mission. Our mission to carry the gospel to a lost and dying world is the intent of the Great Commission. At the heart of the Great Commission is worship of Jesus. William Temple once said:

> The world can be saved by one thing and that is worship. For to worship is to quicken the conscience by the holiness of God, to feed the mind with the truth of God, to purge the imagination by the beauty of God, to open the heart to the love of God, to devote the will to the purpose of God.[2]

The Holy Spirit equips, fills, energizes, and empowers worshippers to declare the wonders of God to the heathen. Psalm 96: 2b–3 states: "Proclaim the good news of His salvation from day to day" (v. 2b NKJV) and "Declare his glory among the heathen, his wonders among all people" (v. 3 KJV).

There are many people around us who are busy about evangelism and yet never bow their knee or lift their hands in worship. They are busy *doing* ministry. There are some who sing songs and lift their hands and yet never share the gospel with their neighbors. They are

---

[2] Robert Morgan, *Preacher's Sourcebook of Creative Sermon Illustrations* (Nashville: Thomas Nelson, 2007), 807.

in love with worship. A worshipping saint (one who has completely fallen in love with Jesus), one who loves Jesus for all that He is and all that He does (one who thoroughly understands the transformational power of worship), will always engage in evangelism. It is totally impossible for the person who truly worships in spirit and truth not to demonstrate the wonder of God in their life.

Great Commission Worshippers are *missional* on two levels: (1) They take the gospel to the nations. Great Commission Worshippers seek to make disciples of Jesus by compelling people to become worshippers of the living Lord, sharing their faith, promoting His wonders, preaching the good news, and proclaiming the glory of God. (2) Great Commission Worshippers reach out to the needy, feed the hungry, care for the sick, embrace the marginalized, take in orphans, love widows, and accept the unwanted. Quoting the apostle Paul's letter to the Roman believers:

> Be kindly affectionate, . . . not lagging in diligence, fervent in spirit, serving the Lord; rejoicing in hope, patient in tribulation, continuing steadfastly in prayer; distributing to the needs of the saints, given to hospitality. Bless those who persecute you; bless and do not curse. (Rom 12:10a,11–14 NKJV)

Great Commission Worshippers become the hands and feet of Jesus. They are driven by passion for God and love for others. They internalize the Great Commission with such conviction that it literally becomes their life's mission. Obedience to that mission is driven by a deep love for Jesus. *Great Commission worshippers are missional.* (See diagram 1 on page 53.)

5. Great Commission worship is **reproducible**. Our goal is to promote and bring into the body of Christ (the church) citizens from every tribe, tongue, culture, nation, or people group. Why? So that they can become worshippers, too!

> My son, be strong in the grace that is in Christ Jesus. And the things that you have heard from me among many witnesses, commit these to faithful men who will be able to teach others

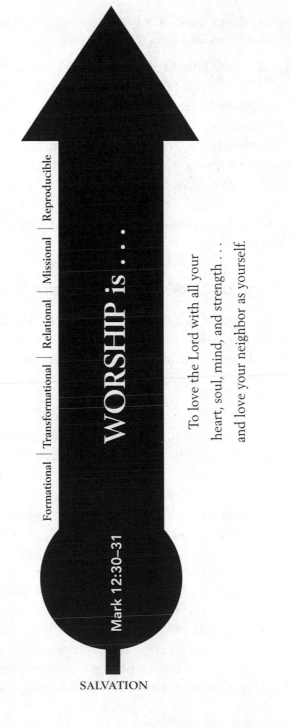

WORSHIP is . . .

Formational | Transformational | Relational | Missional | Reproducible

To love the Lord with all your heart, soul, mind, and strength . . . and love your neighbor as yourself.

Mark 12:30–31

SALVATION

Diagram 1. Model for Worship

also. You therefore must endure hardship as a good soldier of
Jesus Christ. (2 Tim 2:1–3 NKJV)

The mandate is to go into all the world and make fully devoted
followers of Christ—worshippers. This is putting feet on the
missional aspect of Great Commission worship. Discipleship is
critical to the success of Great Commission worship. We become
part of the transformational process as we teach, train, develop, and
nurture new worshippers. Contextualization becomes reality. We
relate our message to culture. We live out in our daily routine lifestyle
evangelism and worship. We communicate the Word of God by the
way we live. *Great Commission worship is **reproducible.*** (See diagram
1 on page 53.)

The Prerequisite for Great Commission Worship

*God is in the process of perfecting you and me for the task of Great
Commission worship.* There are prerequisites involved in formational,
transformational, relational, missional, and reproducible worship
evangelism. What are these prerequisites for Great Commission
worship?

Humility. I often tell my students that they cannot become
the leaders God has called them to be until they first enjoy serving.
Humility is the first prerequisite for Great Commission worship. God
is looking for servant-leaders who demonstrate complete and utter
dependence on Him as sovereign. God wants those whom He places
in leadership roles to see that He alone is Jehovah Jireh.

The word *humble* actually means to demote or lower yourself in
your own estimation, eyes, and ego. Peter, in writing in his epistle to
the churches that were suffering extreme and daily persecution, says,
*"Humble yourselves [themselves] under the mighty hand of God, that He
may exalt you in due time"* (1 Pet 5:6 NKJV).

Two important words are related to humility: *exalt* and *time.* God
is the one who *exalts* people to strategic positions. Remember, God is
sovereign. He gives favor to those whom He chooses. The old prophet
said, *the Most High God is sovereign over all kingdoms on earth and sets*

over them anyone He wishes (see Dan 5:21b). *Exalt* is a transitive verb that means to praise, laud, promote or show great esteem.

We live in a generation that seeks fame. Every generation and every culture and subculture is filled with people who seek to exalt themselves over others. In fact, our postmodern, self-gratifying culture does not look upon humility as a quality or demonstration of strength. The humble are often overlooked, jeered, ridiculed, scorned, and mocked. But humility is a prerequisite for success as a Great Commission Worshipper. God gives grace to those who humble themselves under His mighty hand. God is looking for servant-leaders. Remember, the emphasis is on serving.

The second word associated with humility is *time*. This generation is an impatient group. They have grown accustomed to getting things done with instant speed. And, they quickly grow impatient when things are not delivered with speed and efficiency. Waiting is not part of their mode of operation.

God works in His time. He is not subject to agendas or fast-paced, self-centered clocks. God is in charge, and He exalts a person to strategic positions at the right time, the right moment, and for just the right set of circumstances.

Years ago, I was a candidate for a job with a rather large music publishing company. I think at one point the job was mine for the asking. I saw myself as the most qualified person for the assigned tasks. I had years of experience and the personality type most needed for the position. At least that is what I thought. Somewhere during the course of the interview it became rather obvious that my motives in applying for the job might not have been exactly in line with the organization's mission. Actually, I was in a job I hated. I worked for a man who could at times be most unpredictable and unpleasant. My desire to get out of that really tough working environment clouded my ability to see the realities and nuances of the job for which I was applying. I remember the fellow interviewing me saying somewhere during the evaluative process, "You know, God exalts people in His time. Maybe this isn't the time for you to have this job." He was right.

I didn't get the job. That one decision may have been one of the best things that ever happened to me. I went back home, examined my own motives and disposition, regrouped, and stayed in that ministry until it was God's time for me to move. God will exalt in His time. When He exalts someone, it is always the best time.

Hand of God. The second prerequisite for Great Commission worship involves trusting the mighty hand of God. This too requires submission to the authority and control of God's hand. The apostle's wording is exact: *"Therefore humble yourselves under the mighty hand of God"* (1 Pet 5:6a NKJV). The use of a metaphor—hand—helps us see past the immediate and gaze for a moment into the heart and purposes of our Almighty God. This does not happen until we trust His hand for strength, wisdom, power, guidance, and direction. What happens when we can not *see* God's hand? We trust His heart—His motives, His desire for our lives. Charles H. Spurgeon, the great English preacher of the nineteenth century, put it this way: "God is too good to be unkind. He is too wise to be confused. If I cannot trace His hand, I can always *trust His heart.*"

Trusting God! This is where our worship is best evidenced, revealed, and demonstrated—to the Lord and to those around us. When we surrender to Him to take our lives and do what He wills and knows is best for us, God initiates a process of open communication. Submission to His will, work, and worship prepares opportunity for God to take us to the next step in His relationship with us; in His willingness to *trust us* with bigger and better tasks; and, in revealing to us His plan for our lives. God delights in us. His heart is blessed when He provides and cares for us. He loves to love on us. Why? We belong to Him. God validates and proves His love to us simply because we are His. The more we submit ourselves to His control (His mighty hand), the more He dishes out His love for us. The more we demonstrate our trust in His ability to care for us—by directing our paths, providing our needs, opening doors of opportunity, placing us in strategic positions of influence and opportunity—the more He reveals to us His all-sufficient power to meet our every need. This is especially true when we submit ourselves to Him in worship.

Our humility is most evidenced by our submission. It is only as we submit control of our lives to His mighty hand that we can experience and enjoy lifestyle worship. It is the hand of God that initiates formational worship. It is the almighty hand of God that transforms us into servant leaders—leaders who can teach, train, encourage and edify others to be transformational worshippers. Only the hand of God can build a relationship that lasts for eternity—a relationship with God, fellow believers, and those who know not the love and power of our infinite God. It is by God's hand that His mission to reach the nations is mobilized—making worshippers first at home and then around the globe. Our submission to the hand of God provides a platform for reproductive worship—the final product of a fully devoted servant of the Most High God.

Honor. The third prerequisite for Great Commission worship involves honor. We live in a culture that screams, "Look at me. Look at what I can do." The Bible's admonishment is so contrary to contemporary thought: "Don't praise yourself. Let someone else do it. Let the praise come from a stranger and not from your own mouth" (Prov 27:2 NCV). Just as we live in a culture that seeks bigger and better opportunity, we live in an environment that is obsessed with the idea of marketing, self-promotion, and making other people accept us and what we do. A. W. Tozer puts it into perspective this way:

> There is no limit to what can be done—if it doesn't matter who gets the credit. . . . No man is worthy to succeed until he is willing to fail. No man is morally worthy of success in religious activities until he is willing that the honor of succeeding should go to another if God so wills.

God is the one who exalts and honors His children. Our task is to prepare ourselves for that to which God has called us and then wait on Him to open the door of opportunity. *Honor* in this sense is a transitive verb meaning to esteem someone or something. We honor when we exalt, pay tribute, respect, admire, or dignify someone or something. *Exalt*, on the other hand, is when we promote or raise somebody in rank, position, or esteem. In short, there is no room for self-promotion for the Great Commission Worshipper. Our job? Promote the Lord. He will do the rest.

Honesty. The final prerequisite for Great Commission worship involves honesty. This is an area most often overlooked by those seeking to be obedient to the will of God. It involves personal sincerity, truthfulness, and integrity. We must be honest about calling, our commitment to humility, and, in the process, be patient to let another provide honor. God sees the heart. He knows the motive. He rewards accordingly with opportunity, approval, and success.

Preparing Our Hearts

Before we actually put the hand to the plow and start our work, it is important that our hearts are prepared for the task. Remember the quote by Bob MacKenzie: "The longer the line of preparation, the greater the opportunity." It is important to remember that God is the one who prepares us for the dual tasks of worship and evangelism.

Peter reminds the older saints that they are to nurture and edify the younger leaders in ministry. He then turns his attention to exhorting those who are younger in ministry. He concludes this process by saying, *"But may the God of all grace, who called us to His eternal glory by Christ Jesus, after you have suffered a while, perfect, establish, strengthen, and settle you"* (1 Pet 5:10a NKJV). Here, he outlines the points of preparation, including those that are necessary for Great Commission worship:

He perfects. God is in the process of perfecting you and me. He wants to refine, hone, improve, and sharpen our abilities and talents and in the process faithfully develop our skills for His glory. This is a process. His sweet, precious Holy Spirit is actively working in each of us. As we faithfully seek God's direction, counsel, and guidance, He seeks to conform us to His image, temper our dispositions, smooth out any rough areas in our personalities, give us vision for ministry, and school us in righteousness. It takes time for God to perfect us. Sometimes, He perfects us in areas where we are most vulnerable, self-conscious, and insecure. At other times, He perfects us in areas in which we seem the most confident and self-assured. All in all, He works at shaping our lives so that we can trust in Him to do His good work in us.

He establishes. God is also in the process of establishing us—personally and professionally. By so doing, God proves, confirms, and verifies us and our work—all for His glory. This is where humbling ourselves *under the mighty hand of God* is most important. Why? If we experience any measure of success, our first and greatest temptation will be to brag on the things we can do, totally ignore the reality that God is the one who brings success, and in the process become boastful. All of us deal with this temptation.

The psalmist makes this request of the Lord: "*May the favor of the Lord our God rest on us; establish the work of our hands for us—yes, establish the work of our hands*" (Ps 90:17 NIV). When God establishes our work, He exalts and vindicates our efforts. He demonstrates His favor upon all that we do. He brings success. This is where we can literally delight in the provisions of our Lord the most. When we do, the pressure of success is not our worry. Success becomes a Holy Spirit activity.

He strengthens. This too is a ministry of the Holy Spirit in our lives. When the Holy Spirit strengthens, He reinforces our spiritual graces, fortifies our ability to resist the evil one, and intensifies our spiritual insights. Intellectually, He gives us insight and wisdom. Physically, He makes us stronger, provides endurance for the journey, and health along the way. Emotionally, the Holy Spirit brings peace and comfort during times of struggle. Mentally, He gives abilities to comprehend and remember details. Spiritually, the Holy Spirit gives us grace for success.

He settles. Occasionally, my students will become anxious about an exam or series of assignments given at the beginning of a semester. Invariably, I will find it necessary to remind them that they need to chill, calm down, and relax. The final area of preparation involves resting in the presence of the Lord. Again, God is the one who settles our spirit. He alone is the one who brings peace to an anxious heart.

God doesn't necessarily want us to stop or cease from that which He has called us to do, but He does want us to rest in Him. Remember His promises—to perfect, establish, and strengthen. We need to allow God to calm our spirits. Remember that we need to find our peace, contentment, and consolation in Him.

Our preparation for performance is where the rubber meets the road. It is not enough simply to plan the work. Now, it's time to work our plan. Many times we are busy about planning, but the planning portion is only half the responsibility of good leadership. Putting that plan into action is the best endorsement of the planning process.

We do live in an incredible time of church history. With the introduction and growth of the information age, advancements in technology, and this generation's commitment to social networking, we have opportunity to promote, develop, and participate in evangelism, church growth, worship, and discipleship as never before. We have opportunity to lead God's people in worship unlike any other generation. We have an opportunity to reach out to a dying world with the truth of God's Word. We can make a difference. In the process God uses us as Great Commission Worshippers to change the world.

Principles about Great Commission Worship from This Chapter

We are part of a new paradigm for worship in the evangelical community. God is using worship as a means for evangelism unlike any time in history. Our calling, life experience, educational pursuits, and career opportunities all impact the way we view these changes in worship presentation.

We have discovered that God has called each of us to be a Great Commission Worshipper. The Great Commission is formational, transformational, relational, missional, and reproducible. All of these areas essentially serve as *performance outcomes* for those of us in ministry.

God wants to use each of us to fulfill His purposes. *God is in the process of perfecting you and me for the task of Great Commission worship.* In fact, He wants us to be Great Commission Worshippers. His prerequisites for Great Commission worship are humility, trusting the mighty hand of God, honor, and honesty.

God is the one who prepares us for the task of Great Commission worship. Let's remember that when God calls us to serve, He obligates Himself to equip us. When He obligates Himself to equip, He obligates Himself to provide in every area. So, it is God who perfects, establishes, strengthens, and settles a person, a work, or a ministry for His glory and for the testimony of Jesus Christ.

In our next chapter, we will begin learning how to work our plan as Great Commission Worshippers. Great Commission worship is formational.

Discussion Questions

1. Explain how your "calling" and "experiences" impact your lifestyle of worship and evangelism.

2. Explain how your "education" and "opportunities" impact your lifestyle of worship and evangelism.

3. Of the five "outcomes" of worship, which one do you struggle with the most?

4. Discuss the importance of humility in becoming a Great Commission Worshipper. Are you a humble worshipper? What does it look like to be humble?

5. Discuss the four steps in preparing our hearts to become Great Commission Worshippers? Which step is most difficult for you?

CHAPTER 4

Great Commission Worship Is Formational

*Worship is more than sitting in a pew as a spectator
while the musicians and pastor perform. . . . Worship is
an attitude of heart, mind, and spirit.*

Herschel Hobbs[1]

The preparation for worship studied in chapter 3 provides a platform for demonstrating how worship of God and the work we do for God shape our character, build integrity, and mold our testimony. They are formational. Our worship and evangelism must be based on solid biblical theology and doctrine. Our lives will be different if the worship we do and the evangelism we give ourselves to are biblical. Simply put, our time with God sculpts, forms, and shapes us.

Formational Worship Is a Two-Way Street

We give our worship to God. In response, God nurtures, develops, and cultivates the relationship we have with Him. In this sense, we

---

[1] Hershel H. Hobbs, *My Favorite Illustrations* (Nashville: B&H, 1990), 273.

experience both the transcendence and immanence of our Holy God. Theologians sometimes argue over these terms, but we will use the terms to describe the type of relationship we have in worship of God. First, God is transcendent. This means He is above all. He is the ruler of the universe. He is beyond our limit of experience. God is great and marvelous, magnificent and holy, sufficient and self-sustaining, beyond our own ability even to understand or explain, and Creator of all things (the list can go on and on).[2] We worship Him in all His power. Second, we worship an immanent or providential God.[3] This is the part of God that actively takes a role in our lives. He loves us. He nurtures us. He provides for us. He is our father, our friend, our companion, our hope, and our help (the list can go on and on). Both the concepts of transcendence and immanence are used in this context to describe our relationship with a holy, all-knowing, all-loving God.

The connection we have with God is not a "one-way" relationship. God does not just receive our worship as some type of gift package, bundle it up in a great, big storage unit in the sky, and at the end of the day make a list accounting for the number of times we pray, exalt Him, and brag on His goodness and mercy in some way. God is not selfish. He does not need us to brag on Him. He is not so self-centered as to demand from us "loyal worshippers" some kind of memorized series of drones and prayers. We worship Him as the transcendent, all-knowing, omniscient, omnipresent, and omnipotent God.

When we worship in faith with our love, devotion, obedience, and service, He responds to us. He gives us His grace, love, devotion, companionship, and care. As we spend time with Him in worship, He increases our desire to worship. As He increases that desire, we worship more deeply and sincerely. God uses our worship to shape us and form us into His likeness.

To better understand the principle of formational worship, let's take a moment and look into the life of the Old Testament prophet

---

[2] Scriptural examples that support God's transcendence: Ps 99:3,5,9; Isa 6:3; 40:18–26; 55:8–9; Rev 4:8, etc.

[3] Scriptural examples that support God's immanence: Gen 34:14–15; Jer 29:4–14 NIV; Ps 135:7; Matt 5:45; 10:29–30; Acts 17:27–28; Col 1:16–17, etc.

Jeremiah. Jeremiah was a young man when commissioned by God to carry out the task of telling an ungrateful, ungodly, self-consumed nation that because of their sins they were going to reap grief, destruction, heartache, and devastation.

Nearly a century ago, Mohandas K. Gandhi made the following statement on the seven influences that will destroy a nation, a people, a family, and a life:

> Politics without principle!
> Pleasure without conscience!
> Wealth without work!
> Knowledge without character!
> Business without morality!
> Science without humanity!
> Worship without sacrifice.[4]

Thus was the condition of Judah at the time of Jeremiah's ministry. They practiced politics without principle. Their hearts were given to pleasure without conscience. Generations only understood wealth without work. Even as far back as the reign of King Solomon, they sought knowledge without the guiding force of character. The leaders of Judah gave themselves over to business without morality. For many years they had worshipped without the wonder of the living God in their lives. Their hearts were full of evil, ungodly worship of idols—with all the trappings, including sexual promiscuity, human sacrifice, and demon worship.

Jeremiah's Calling. By his own testimony, Jeremiah was unfit for the task. He lacked the eloquence, persuasiveness, and fluency necessary for such a prestigious position. He was a priest by birth and called by the Lord to be a prophet at the young age of 21. Even though he felt unfit for the task, God had a plan for Jeremiah's life. He told the prophet to "go to everyone I send you to and say whatever I command you." He instructed Jeremiah not to be afraid. He promised sovereign protection and companionship. "For I am with you and will rescue you," declared the Lord. God continues:

---

[4] See http://www.sermonillustrations.com/a-z/e/enemies.htm.

"Get yourself ready! Stand up and say to them whatever I
command you." Do not be terrified by them—the kings of Judah,
its officials, its priests and the people of the land. They will fight
against you but will not overcome you, for I am with you and
will rescue you." (Jer 1:17,18b,19a NIV)

"What God asks us to do he fits us for, and what he fits us for he
asks us to do," wrote Henrietta C. Mears.[5] In spite of his reluctance
to undertake the task, Jeremiah accepted God's calling upon him
as a prophet. God appointed Jeremiah a prophet over nations and
kingdoms. God instructed him to uproot and tear down, destroy and
overthrow, to build and to plant (Jer 1:7b,10).

And prophesy he did. Jeremiah prophesied forthrightly, with fore-
sight and insight, the captivity and restoration of Judah; the destruction of the Gentile nations Moab, Ammon, Edom, Elam, Babylon,
Philistia, and Egypt; the capture and demise of Jerusalem, Babylon,
and Damascus; and the coming Messiah.

The story is told of Donald Grey Barnhouse, the famous theologian and Bible teacher, giving counsel to a young woman on the side-
walk in front of Tenth Presbyterian Church in Philadelphia. It was after
a Sunday evening service that the woman approached Dr. Barnhouse
saying, "I want to follow Christ, but I want to be famous, too." She
had moved to New York with the idea that she was going to pursue a
career in musical theatre. "I'll follow Christ completely," she explained,
"after I have made it in the theatre." The old theologian took a key out
of his pocket and scratched a mark on a nearby postal box. "That is
what God will let you do," he told the girl. "God will let you scratch the
surface of success. He will let you get close enough to the top to know
what it is, but he will never let you have it." Barnhouse explained, "He
will never let one of his children have anything other than himself."

Years later, he met the girl again. She told him how her career had
been full of ups and downs. She had dabbled with limited success—a
small part here and there. She then told Dr. Barnhouse, "I can't tell

---

[5] Henrietta C. Mears, *What the Bible Is All About* (Glendale, CA: Gospel Light,
1966), 242.

you how many times in my discouragement I have closed my eyes and seen you scratching on that postal box with your key." God let the young lady scratch the edges, but He gave her nothing that would take the place of Himself.[6]

Jeremiah's Submission. Jeremiah submitted himself to the mighty hand of God, and through his times of worship, his life was shaped and fashioned. He used metaphors and object lessons as a means for communicating the gospel. Among his many examples are the use of an almond rod (Jer 1:11–12), a full bottle (Jer 13:12–14), a broken bottle (Jer 19:1–2), and hidden stones (Jer 43:9–13). Perhaps his most famous object lesson is found in Jer 18:1–6 (NKJV):

> The word which came to Jeremiah from the LORD, saying: "Arise and go down to the potter's house, and there I will cause you to hear My words." Then I went down to the potter's house, and there he was, making something at the wheel. And the vessel that he made of clay was marred in the hand of the potter; so he made it again into another vessel, as it seemed good to the potter to make. Then the word of the LORD came to me, saying: "O house of Israel, can I not do with you as this potter?" says the LORD. "Look, as the clay *is* in the potter's hand, so *are* you in My hand, O house of Israel!"

My wife loves to go to pottery shops. She likes to look at the sizes, shapes, and colors of the ceramic bowls, cups, and various plates and dishes. She is especially fond of going to the Williamsburg Pottery Factory, just outside of Williamsburg, Virginia. She can watch pottery being made there from Virginia clay. She can actually watch pottery artisans select the clay, create a big ball of material for use on a potter's wheel, and then hand-shape a bowl or vase for use in our home. It is an interesting and fascinating process.

Pottery was a much respected profession in the days of Jeremiah. Today, it encompasses many of the same creative processes that it did centuries ago. Pottery includes earthenware, stoneware, and porcelain.

---

[6] J. M. Boice, *Christ's Call to Discipleship* (Chicago: Moody, 1986), 154.

Pottery is created by shaping a clay body into a required form and heating that figure to a high temperature in an oven, also called a kiln.

Critical in the creative process is the use of clay mixtures from indigenous regions with other minerals. This gives each fixture individuality and character. The chemicals within the clay and minerals react when placed inside the oven.

The most basic tool for the maker of good pottery is the hand. Additional tools such as a potter's wheel, turntables, along with shaping paddles and anvils are often used. Some potters use rolling tools such as roulettes, slab rollers, and rolling pins. Often cutting and piercing tools are used such as knives, wires, and fluting tools. The potter will usually use finishing tools such as burnishing stones, rasps, and chamois to conclude the creative process.

Proper firing is critical to the manufacturing process of good pottery. Only after exposing the clay object to the intense heat can that article be called pottery. This firing or heating process produces irreversible changes in the pottery itself. It induces reaction that strengthens and hardens their shape—often leading to a permanent change. Temperature and time in the kiln are critical to the maturing process of good pottery. Likewise, the oxidizing atmosphere within the kiln can affect the appearance of the finished product.

Finally, the glaze. This is the coating applied to pottery after its first heating. This provides opportunity to render the product waterproof, provide protection, and apply creative decorations and color. After the glaze is applied, the vessel is once again heated before being delivered as a finished product.

The resulting product, after going through this process, can often be remarkable and beautiful. On occasion due to a flaw in the chemical makeup of the clay, problems in the shaping of the vessel, or the firing process, a vessel might turn out defective or flawed. When this happens, the potter has three options: (1) if the vessel has not been exposed to all the fire and heat of a kiln, it can be remolded, reshaped, and reformed into another fixture; (2) if the product has been through the entire process and comes out flawed, the potter can break the vessel into small pieces, grind the glass and materials into powder, and use it in making a totally new vessel; or, (3) throw the vessel away. Interestingly, a vessel reshaped, remolded, and refashioned is often stronger and much more durable than the original vessel with the flaws and distortions.

The process for making pottery shows how God wants to shape us in much the same way as the person crafting and shaping clay into a fine vessel. God wants to shape us into His image. Just like clay in the potter's hand, God wants to fashion our lives into a vessel fit for His service. Our personalities, strengths and weaknesses, likes and dislikes all combine to form clay in the hands of our God. Just as the clay and chemicals react to the fire and environment of a kiln, our worship reveals the character of our reaction to culture, social influences, and love for God. He wants to take our gifts of worship— our hearts of love for God—and shape them into acceptable worship and praise.

God was seeking to reshape the worship of Judah from idolatry back to true love and allegiance of Himself. The longer they worshipped other gods, the weaker they became spiritually, emotionally, physically, and intellectually. They did not know their hearts were empty. They had certainly lost perspective. More importantly, they lost their desire to worship God. They simply went through the motions. Their worship did not emanate from hearts of genuine love for God.

Mildred Witte Struven once said, "A clay pot sitting in the sun will always be a clay pot. It has to go through the white heat of the furnace to become porcelain."[7] Likewise, when our worship is marred by the chemical imbalances of this world, the evil influences of a carnal culture, and the self-centeredness of ego, God must take us and reshape us as new vessels. He places us in the kiln of His Word and then allows us to confront our life experiences—trials, hardship, persecution, and, at times, suffering.

Reggie McNeal explains in his book, *A Work of Heart*, that God shapes our lives through culture, calling, community, communion

---

[7] Mildred Witte Struven, in *Bits and Pieces* (September 19, 1991): 6.

(with the Lord), conflict, and the commonplace experiences we encounter.[8] I add one important ingredient to this list—the work of the Holy Spirit. You see, God places the glaze of the Holy Spirit upon our lives and creates a totally different texture, a new vessel. He reshapes our desires. It is through the working of the Holy Spirit in our lives that we develop the right disposition to be a leader. When God does His work in our lives, our worship begins to take on a different look, a new character. Like pottery refashioned and made anew into a reliable vessel of honor, we too take on new character, develop a reliable finish, and become usable for His kingdom.

Jeremiah's Success. Jeremiah did more than scratch the surface of all that God planned for him. He was known throughout all the lands of Judah for his loyalty and love of the Lord. He prophesied for more than 40 years. God was with Jeremiah every step of the way. He proclaimed the "word of the Lord" before, during, and after the fall of Judah into the hands of Nebuchadnezzar. He predicted a period of 70 years in captivity (Jer 25:13–19). At one point, evil priests and prophets laid hold of Jeremiah and threatened death. They accused him of being unpatriotic. He was imprisoned because of his prophesies against the city of Jerusalem, the king, and the evil practices of idolatry. Yet, God delivered him from his enemies. Through it all, God remembered the promise given to Jeremiah: "'Do not be afraid of them, for I am with you and will rescue you,' declares the LORD" (Jer 1:8 NIV). Oswald Chambers observes:

> God promised Jeremiah that he would deliver him personally.
> That is all God promises His children. Wherever God sends us,
> he will guard our lives. Our personal property and possessions
> are a mater of indifference, we have to sit loosely to all those
> things; if we do not, there will be panic and heartbreak and
> distress. That is the inwardness of the overshadowing of personal
> deliverance.[9]

---

[8] Reggie McNeal, *A Work of Heart: Understanding How God Shapes Spiritual Leaders* (San Francisco, CA: Jossey-Bass, 2000), v.

[9] Oswald Chambers, *My Utmost for His Highest* (London: Dodd, Mead & Co., 1935), 179.

The only child of a temple priest, molded by strong, godly influences and a much-needed revival led by a child-king, Jeremiah's real character demonstrates this genuine love for God and hatred for idol worship. He had distain for the dishonest policies of the monarchs in Judah. His messages were unpopular with the evil kings of Judah and their spiritually blind, evil followers. On more than one occasion he ran for his life. Even so, Jeremiah never lost the sense of his calling. His commitment to the worship of Jehovah shaped a simple, honest, and consistent trust in God. His worship of God was formational.

Just how was Jeremiah's worship formational?

First, God shaped Jeremiah's language. God reached out His hand and touched the prophet's mouth. "Say whatever I command you," God said (Jer 1:7b NIV). "Before I formed you in the womb I knew you, before you were born I set you apart" (Jer 1:5). "See, I am putting my words in your mouth" (Jer 1:9 NCV). The Bible says that God gave Jeremiah the words to say. He will do the same for you and me.

Second, God shaped Jeremiah's love. God shaped Jeremiah's life so that it demonstrated unquestionable love for God as sovereign ruler. His love for God impacted his daily life. The lesson for us? We need to love God with such passion that our worship of God impacts the way we live. As we express our love to God through faithful worship, God, through the person and work of the Holy Spirit, shapes our lives in such a way that we actively demonstrate genuine love for Him in our places of work, communities, and homes. Others see what God is doing in us.

Third, God shaped Jeremiah's life. Jeremiah's worship prompted him to live a life of obedience. His obedience was driven by simple worship. His faith drove him to a life of faithful commitment and service to the one he loved most, the God of the ages. His faithfulness energized his courage to always do right. God used what looked like unbearable circumstances to shape Jeremiah's character, integrity, and faith. In response, Jeremiah deepened his own worship of the Lord.

Consider this: God used Jeremiah when Nebuchadnezzar captured Jerusalem. Nebuchadnezzar's plan to deport the best Jews from Judah to Babylon proved to be a political, social, cultural, and educational stroke of genius. He relocated, repositioned, reestablished, and reorganized the entire working population of Judah. Strategically, it was an economic coup. He took the "best people" from Judah for use in building a superior working class infrastructure for his empire. He fed these new emigrants with food from the best parts of his land. He educated them in all the ways of the Chaldaeans. He sought to integrate them into Babylonian culture. They could only speak Chaldee. He allowed them to build community.

Can you imagine how difficult it might have been for the people of Judah to make the transition to their new homes in Babylon? New family. New homes. New environment. New religion. New schools. New culture. New food, and a new, unkind, disrespectful work environment with supervisors unfamiliar with their Hebrew worship!

God knew they would face these challenges. As part of His instructions to Jeremiah, He told the prophet to comfort His people. "Tell them I already have a plan for them," God said. So, amid a whole series of oracles chiding Judah for their sin, God gave a message to Jeremiah specifically designed for the soon-to-be-emigrant Jews:

> This is what the LORD Almighty, the God of Israel, says to all
> those I carried into exile from Jerusalem to Babylon: "Build
> houses and settle down; plant gardens and eat what they
> produce. Marry and have sons and daughters; find wives for
> your sons and give your daughters in marriage, so that they too
> may have sons and daughters. Increase in number there; do not
> decrease. Also, seek the peace and prosperity of the city to which
> I have carried you into exile. Pray to the LORD for it, because
> if it prospers, you too will prosper." Yes, this is what the LORD
> Almighty, the God of Israel, says: "Do not let the prophets and
> diviners among you deceive you. Do not listen to the dreams
> you encourage them to have. They are prophesying lies to you in
> my name. I have not sent them," declares the LORD. (Jer 29:4–9
> NIV)

Jeremiah was faithful to do what God commanded of him. He told the Judeans God's plan for their own lives. God used this time to work in Jeremiah's life and in the hearts of His people. So, when the people were discouraged, God used Jeremiah to provide courage. When they were hungry, God provided food. When the people were desperate in spirit, God used Jeremiah to communicate peace. In the process, God was honored and His glory was revealed to an ungodly nation.

To every weary soldier, discouraged worshipper, or lonely saint: God desires to work in your life in much the same way. You may have totally lost focus. You care much too much about what other people think about you—your dreams—your ambitions—your successes. Perhaps you've lost the wonder of loving God long ago.

Just like God wanted to use those from Judah as a reflection of His glory, He wants to use you and your life to demonstrate His love and mercy. He wants you to be refreshed by His counsel, His comfort, His companionship, and His care. Maybe you too need to stop, assess things, and renew your relationship with Him. Rekindle your worship of Him. Start over by allowing Him to shape you into the kind of vessel best suited for His purposes.

Fourth, God shaped Jeremiah's labor and work. J. Hudson Taylor (1832–1905) was an English missionary to China. Taylor founded the world-famous China Inland Mission (CIM). At his death, the China Inland ministries included 205 mission stations with more than 800 missionaries and 125,000 Chinese Christian converts. Taylor was a man who had clear-cut convictions about how God's work should be accomplished.

Do we often make our plans and then try to carry them out in our own strength? Are we making plans without God's counsel? Do we go to God with an entitlement attitude and ask Him to "bless these plans"? "Another way of working," explains Hudson Taylor, "is to begin with God; to ask his plans, and to offer ourselves to him to carry out his purposes."[10]

At the moment Jeremiah accepted God's plan for his life, God began to mold, shape, and craft the young prophet into a man of courage. Jeremiah lived and experienced formational worship. God gave him the ability to carry out the task before him:

> Today I am going to make you a strong city, an iron pillar, a bronze wall. You will be able to stand against everyone in the land. . . . They will fight against you, but they will not defeat you, because I am with you to protect you!" says the LORD. (Jer 1:18a–19 NCV)

Jeremiah relied on this promise his entire life. He experienced the favor of the Lord and God was faithful to every promise, word, and obligation made to the prophet. His worship of God shaped his labor for God.

Jeremiah was chosen from his youth to be a prophet of the Most High God. As God breathed upon Jeremiah, the prophet wrote down the word of the Lord. Each time the prophet received a word from God, his understanding about God grew, his theology of God developed, his worship of God deepened, and his life was shaped through the process. As Jeremiah honored God, the Lord God honored the prophet.

Biblical Theology Is Formational

Theology is the study of God. What we believe about God shapes and forms everything we believe. Obviously, theology, Scripture, and doctrine are somewhat interchangeable in application. But, as we spend time in worship of God and study of His truth, we learn more about God. As we spend more time with God, He uses His Word to guide us in the understanding of doctrine—what we believe. As we

---

[10] W. Wiersbe, *Wycliffe Handbook of Preaching and Preachers* (Chicago: Moody, 1984), 243.

understand doctrine, the Lord speaks to our hearts about how we should apply truth to daily living.

What we believe about God shapes and fashions our entire belief system. We make application to life almost solely on the basis of what we believe. Another way to say it is like this:

THEOLOGY = PHILOSOPHY = METHODOLOGY

As we spend time in worship of God, He reveals more and more about Himself. Our understanding of God is enlightened. Our love for the Lord is enlarged. Our obedience of His Word is energized. The more we know about God (our theology), the more our philosophy (or doctrine) in life is shaped. Our philosophy determines how we might apply truth to daily living (methodology).

How does this play out in our regular routine of worship and evangelism? Perhaps this illustration can help explain the principle:

I learn from God's Word that God wants all people from all nations to worship Him and that salvation is available to all people groups in all the world. My theology tells me that all people need to be worshippers of the Most High God. My philosophy tells me that I need to develop a personal strategy for telling people how to become worshippers of God. My methodology—the application—motivates me to participate in one-on-one opportunities to share the gospel.

God is sovereign. He knows what we need to know in order to understand more about Him. He knows what we need in our hearts when we step out in faith to tell someone about the love of the Lord. He knows how our lips need to be prepared to proclaim His story to lost men and women. He knows exactly how to take what we know about Him (our theology) and translate it into language that the average unsaved person can understand. Keep in mind that our theology of God often:

- Shapes our thinking about God as Creator, Sustainer, Ruler, and King.
- Shapes our knowledge of God's majesty and power.
- Shapes our understanding of God's glory.
- Shapes our love for God and His mercy, grace, and forgiveness.

- Shapes our rationale for service.
- Shapes our discernment for obedience.

Scripture Is Formational

The Jewish psychiatrist Victor Frankl was arrested and imprisoned by the Nazis in World War II. Stripped of everything he owned—family possessions, his writing and property—he had spent years writing a book on the importance of finding life's meaning. Upon arrival at the concentration camp, Auschwitz, he hid his treasured manuscript in the lining of his coat. The Nazis forced everyone in the camp to give up their clothes. To Frankl's horror, he lost his manuscript and the only record he possessed for any kind of intellectual or emotional comfort. He began asking himself if "life was ultimately void of any meaning." He lost hope. In time, the Nazis handed Frankl another set of clothing.

"Instead of the many pages of my manuscript," Frankl wrote later, "I found in the pocket of the newly acquired coat a single page torn out of a Hebrew prayer book." Written on that single page were the words of the *Shema Yisrael*, the Jewish confession of faith. Taken from Deut 6:4–9, it reads: "Hear, O Israel! The Lord our God is one God. And you shall love the Lord your God with all your heart and with all your soul and with all your might."

This was no coincidence. God was teaching Victor Frankl how to live His thoughts and heart desires. God was instilling in Frankl's heart a reason to survive. He was giving the philosopher the understanding and the knowledge that there is a meaning in one's life. Later, as Frankl reflected on his experience, he wrote: "He who has a why to live for can bear almost any how."[11]

God gave them hope and He will give you hope, too. He will give you a purpose for life. He will reveal His own purposes for you. God uses His Word to teach us about Himself. The Bible says:

> For the word of God is living and active. Sharper than any
> double-edged sword, it penetrates even to dividing soul and

---

[11] See http://www.sermonillustrations.com/a-z/s/suffering.htm.

spirit, joints and marrow; it judges the thoughts and attitudes
of the heart. Nothing in all creation is hidden from God's sight.
Everything is uncovered and laid bare before the eyes of him to
whom we must give account. (Heb 4:12–13 NIV)

The use of "sharper than any double-edged sword" is an
interesting metaphor to describe the work of the Word of God. Most
often, when referring to the use of a "sword" in Christian disciplines,
our thoughts immediately go to our responsibility to put on the "full
armor of God" in Eph 6:17: "take . . . the sword of the Spirit, which
is the Word of God." Certainly, our battle is not against people (flesh
and blood) but against the rulers and authorities and the powers of
this world's darkness, and spiritual powers of evil. The use of "sword"
in Hebrews 4 seems to imply a different application: First, the sword
functions much like a surgeon's scalpel. The doctor carefully locates
the place for surgery, makes an incision, penetrates deep into flesh
to the place for treatment, and skillfully uses his scalpel to cut out
and remove infection or diseased tissue. Second, the sword may be
used as a tool for clearing away rough edges and shaping an object
into a desired image—not at all unlike the use of tools in shaping and
forming expensive pottery.

The Word of God is formational. Just like the scalpel in the hand
of a skilled doctor or the anvil in the hands of a talented maker of
pottery, God uses His Word to shape and develop our worship. As we
spend time with Him in His Word, our worship is shaped by what we
read and the Holy Spirit enables us to worship Him even better. In
the process, our lives, relationships, ministries, and efforts are shaped
by our worship.

Doctrine Is Formational

We are shaped by doctrine. Doctrine has everything to do with what
we believe. As we are shaped by the Word of God and as we learn
how to apply His truth to daily life through worship, we find that the
Holy Spirit develops a deep, satisfying set of beliefs in our own heart.
These are norms or convictions that help shape our values, guide us

through the day, establish relationships, and provide passion as we serve the Lord. The more time we spend in God's Word, on our knees in prayer, and practicing worship, the more we are influenced and changed. In the end, worship and doctrine are much like faith—once the process begins, they become cyclical.

Our study of God's Word shapes our worship. The more we worship, the more we establish a clear, definable set of doctrines. The more the Holy Spirit changes our belief system, the more we want to know of the Bible. The more time we spend in His Word, the more we want to know about God. The more we understand about God, the more we want to worship. The more we worship, the more the Holy Spirit enables us to establish a dogma for living. Maybe you get the picture.

American Indians had an exceptional ritual in the training of young braves. On the morning of a boy's thirteenth birthday, the father and son practiced and refined their skill of hunting, scouting, and fishing. As evening approached, the boy was put to a final test. He was blindfolded and taken several miles away and placed in a dense forest to spend the entire night—alone. Upon taking the blindfold off, he would find that he was in the middle of a thick forest. The idea was for the young, soon-to-be warrior to stay in that one spot until morning came. Every snapping of a twig, rustling of the wind, movement of the night only left the young man full of fear—wondering if a wild animal would pounce upon his small body. Obviously, the night forest had the potential of casting fear upon the young man's heart. After what often seemed like an eternity, dawn would break. Looking around, the boy would see the trees, flowers, sunlight slipping through the forest, and a well-worn path. To his amazement, he would also see his father, armed with a bow and arrow, just a few feet away. His father had been there all along. During the night the young boy could not see his father, but the father never lost sight of his son.[12]

---

[12] *Our Daily Bread*, http://www.sermonillustrations.com/a-z/p/protection.htm.

In many ways, the work of the Holy Spirit serves us in much the same way as the Indian father in this short story. As we study God's Word while we worship, the Holy Spirit watches over us, teaching, training, shaping, and molding us into the kind of Great Commission worshippers we need to be for the kingdom of God. The Holy Spirit protects us from evil forces that might influence our thinking. As we feed on God's Word and engage in worship, the Holy Spirit shapes our minds and hearts, opens our eyes to truth, and prompts us to apply truth to what eventually becomes our own personal doctrine.

Theology, Scripture, and doctrine—which comes first? I'm not altogether sure which comes first for the Great Commission Worshipper. God uses all three to facilitate our understanding of Himself. Certainly as we worship God in spirit and truth, as we unselfishly reach out to those around us in love with the gospel, and as we seek to live a lifestyle that reflects the glory of God, we find that our lives are shaped, formed, and fashioned into the image of Christ. It definitely is a process. That process takes time.

Principles about Great Commission Worship from This Chapter

So, how are worship and evangelism formational?

First, formational worship is a two-way relationship. God always responds to our worship. As we worship our transcendent, almighty, sovereign God, our Lord responds by showing Himself as an immanent, personal, loving, and gracious father. He shapes us as we worship. He conforms us to His will as we submit ourselves to His authority and control over our lives. He fashions us into His image as we seek to know more about Him.

Second, formational worship shapes our calling, defines our submission, and determines our successes. In the life of Jeremiah, God used worship as a means to form and shape what he would say. God used Jeremiah's worship to shape the love the prophet had for God and the love he had for the Hebrew people. He told the prophet to go to the potter and observe the *formational process.*

Jeremiah learned that God uses all parts of the creative process for His glory: the clay mixtures—each individual is different; the tools—in the hands of a skilled potter (which in this case was God Himself); the fire—for refining and clearing out all impurities; the glaze—the work of the Holy Spirit.

God also used Jeremiah's commitment to worship in shaping his concept about life. He taught Jeremiah the importance of contextualization in worship, and his worship impacted his own labor and work.

Third, formational worship is based on theology (understanding of God), **Scripture** (God's revealed truth), **and doctrine** (our belief system upon which we base our life philosophy).

God uses theology to clarify our understanding of Himself as God. He uses Scripture as a means of revealing Himself to us in greater, richer, and more meaningful ways. Always remember that the Word of God is alive and active. It is sharper than any double-edged sword. God's Word penetrates even to dividing soul and spirit, joints and marrow. God uses His Word to judge the thoughts and attitudes of our hearts. As we read God's Word and worship Him alone, His Holy Spirit begins to teach us.

God uses our understanding of Scripture and commitment to honest, biblical theology as a means for establishing doctrine. God is glorified as we formulate and build our philosophy for living in accordance with the Word of God. God is blessed as we develop methodology for reaching out to a desperate, dying world with the gospel and compelling others to become worshippers of the living Lord.

In our next chapter, we will see how worship is transformational. God is in the business of changing our lives. He alone has the power to change hearts, reform a nation, and transform chaos into peace.

Discussion Questions

1. Explain how formational worship is a two-way street. How does that impact you?

2. Discuss Jeremiah's approach to formational worship. Which point of Jeremiah's approach can you relate to the most?

3. Discuss how biblical theology is formational. Why is this important?

4. Discuss how holy Scripture is formational in the life of the believer. Why is this important?

5. Fully discuss the implications of doctrine being formational in a Christian's spiritual development as a Great Commission Worshipper.

CHAPTER 5

Great Commission Worship Is Transformational

> *Worship liberates the personality by giving a new perspective to life, by integrating life with the multitude of life-forms, by bringing into the life the virtues of humility, loyalty, devotion and rightness of attitude, thus refreshing and reviving the spirit.*
>
> Roswell C. Long[1]

W orship is transformational. God is in the business of changing people. We teach, train, encourage, edify, and share the gospel with the lost for the sole purpose of seeing God do His work in the lives of men and women, boys and girls. The Holy Spirit is in the business of transforming lives from old to new, dead to living, hurting and broken to healed and recreated. This is the call of evangelism, and in the process God takes a broken person and transforms him or her into a worshipper of God.

---

[1] Hershel H. Hobbs, *My Favorite Illustrations* (Nashville: Broadman and Holman, 1990), 271.

In our last chapter, we discussed the important role worship has in shaping, molding, nurturing, and maturing our lives. Worship is formational, but worship is also transformational. Authentic worship of Jesus changes a person.

Change is a fascinating word. "Change" is used as a verb 26 times in 23 verses in the Old and New Testaments. In the Greek text, it means to "change the figure or to be transformed." As a transitive or an intransitive verb, it means to pass from one state to another, substitute or replace something, or become different. As a noun, "change" involves "making or becoming different, varying from routine, or transition from one stage or phase to another."

The word *changed* is used 43 times in 42 verses in the Bible. The Greek transliteration of *changed* simply means "to cause one thing to cease and another to take its place." This is the word used in 1 and 2 Corinthians and Hebrews when dealing with the change that takes place when we are transformed at the resurrection.[2] While the word *change* or *changed* is not used in 2 Cor 5:17, the kind of renovation we are talking about when we refer to transformational worship is certainly implied: *If anyone belongs to Christ, there is a new creation. The old things have gone; everything is made new!* (2 Cor 5:17 NCV).

Let's consider this process of transformation a bit. Certainly, it involves change, but there is more to be considered. Perhaps words like *renovate, convert, restore, switch, mend,* and even *re-establish* or *refurbish* communicate this *transformation* principle. Our worship (our demonstration of love for God, our adoration of God, our exaltation of God) should be so engaging, personal, defining that when we leave God's presence, we are different. Sometimes the change is immediately evident—like when we experience the burden lift as we repent of our sins. At other times, the change is gradual and not evidenced except over a period of time. Either way, the Holy Spirit executes change in our lives as we worship in spirit and truth.

Be assured, it's not the worship songs we sing that transform our lives. It's not the prayers we pray, the sermons we deliver, the engaging

---

[2] 1 Cor 15:51–52; 2 Cor 3:18; Heb 1:12.

and moving video about missions we watch, the offerings we bring, the invitations we give, or the testimony we share that transforms our lives. Transformation only comes when the Lord receives our songs, prayers, sermons, offerings, testimonies, and services as sincere, honest, personal gifts of love for Him—and to Him! If our ceremony of worship transformed our lives, worship would become mere ritual. The Holy Spirit transforms our lives, not our actions, service, sacrament, or formal procedure for worship.

Actually, our *acts* of worship don't do anything to change us. It is during worship that the Holy Spirit begins to break down the bitterness, anger, self-promoting attitudes, and the spirit of greed in our hearts. And, it is this kind of transformation that changes a life, family, church, and nation.

It is this kind of transformational worship that Jacob experienced at Bethel. He wrestled with God all night. In the morning, he was transformed into a different person. His hatred for his older brother was gone. His spirit of deception and self-centeredness was gone. His attitude about what God wanted him to do was forever changed. His name was changed to Israel. God marked Jacob with a crippled hip, and his relationship with his older brother, Esau, was restored. Jacob was transformed as he worshipped the Lord (Gen 32:22–31).

Jonah experienced transformation while in the belly of the fish. He repented of his selfishness. He began to reconsider his own misguided motives. I'm certain that he captured a new vision of who God is and of His awesomeness. While parked somewhere between that fish's lungs, heart, and intestines, Jonah was transformed (Jonah 1–2).

Ezekiel was transformed by his worship. The bashful, somewhat backward prophet was transformed as he saw the glory of the Lord (Ezek 1:28). His ambitions were changed when he felt the hand of the Lord upon him (Ezek 1:3; 3:14,22). In spite of his attempt to resist God's call on his life, Ezekiel obeyed God and was transformed through worship. DiAnna Paulk observed Ezekiel's encounter with *God's glory* to be a life-changing experience:

It is one thing to understand the concept of God's glory, but Ezekiel was able to see it and feel it and taste it and hear it. He experienced God's glory![3]

Ezekiel fell on his face and worshipped. The experience forever changed his life. The reoccurring experience proved to be the resource which fueled his ministry. It was the one source the prophet turned to time and time again. The glory of God was there when his wife suddenly died, when he observed the wheel in the middle of the wheel, in the middle of the desert to witness the gathering of dry bones, and to see the prophecy of God's people fully restored in fellowship with a holy God. God permitted Ezekiel to see as much of His glory as the prophet's emotions could tolerate, endure, or bear. The experience forever transformed the way he thought, worshipped, and served God. The experience changed him as person. He began to see the Lord and the things of God in the reality of eternity. Ezekiel was forever transformed as he worshipped the living Lord.

Saul was forever transformed on the road to Damascus as he worshipped Jesus. Like Jacob centuries before, he emerged from the experience with a new name—Paul. We don't know exactly what Paul saw in the heavens, but it changed his life and his perspective. Like Ezekiel, it gave him the motivation, power, energy, and incentive to do all that God had called him to do. The apostle Paul never got over the transformational worship experienced on the Damascus highway. The moment he encountered Jesus, Paul was forever changed, and today we are the recipients of the work and ministry God accomplished in his life. At least 13 of the New Testament books were penned by Paul.

Peter experienced transformational worship. One would think that Peter's experience of walking on the water would have been his defining moment with Jesus. After all, Jesus got into the boat, calmed the sea, and they worshipped Him. What about the time Peter saw Moses, Elijah, and Abraham with Jesus on the Mount of

---

[3] DiAnna Paulk (http://www.path-light.com/E01glory.htm).

Transfiguration? Surely that would have been the moment Peter experienced transformational worship. Transformational worship must have taken place when Peter repented of denying Christ during the days of the crucifixion. No. Peter's transformation came on the day that 120 gathered together in an upper room and they were filled with the Holy Ghost (Acts 2:1–41). It was when Peter and the others were in the middle of a focused time of worship that God fulfilled His promise and blessed them with His presence. At that moment, Peter experienced transformational worship and was forever changed.

Isaiah and Transformational Worship

Consider Isaiah. Isaiah's worship was transformational. His worship was deeply personal, moving, and life-changing. Isaiah was a pre-exilic prophet to the country of Judah—the southern kingdom. Isaiah was a man of great vision and confidence about his own time, the imminent captivity of Judah, and the coming of Jesus Christ as King of kings.

Isaiah was a young aristocrat. He was from a princely line. Brought up in the court, he had the respect of the Jerusalem constituency. He lived during the time when the northern kingdom (the ten northern tribes of Israel) were devastated by the Assyrians. He prophesied against the Assyrian king and spoke with conviction about the arrogance displayed by that ungodly, vile nation (Isa 10:5–34).

Married to a prophetess (8:3,18), Isaiah foretold how God was going to carry out His purposes through the Messiah. During the reigns of Uzziah; briefly under Jotham; Ahaz—a wicked idolatrous monarch; and, Hezekiah—a godly man who sought to remove idolatry from the land, Isaiah proclaimed the truth about the Messiah establishing His kingdom over the whole earth.

The Criteria for Worship (1:11–19)

In every college degree, there are upper level courses that require a certain number of prerequisites. These involve basic, fundamental, nut-and-bolt information or knowledge required to begin study in a specific discipline or course of study. In music, one must have a clear understanding of music theory before proceeding to the study of composition; in medicine, one must demonstrate an understanding of basic biology before proceeding to microbiology; or, in counseling, a student must have basic psychology and sociology before moving on to advanced counseling courses. In Isaiah 1, God provides some prerequisites for transformational worship.

First, cease and desist (1:11–15,16b). Isaiah tells the people of Judah that God does not want their false sacrifices. He tells them that God hates their incense, emphasis on new moons, Sabbath, and other feast days. He explains how God cannot stand the evil they do in their holy meetings. He then tells them that because of their murderous practices that they need to stop raising their arms in prayer. God is not listening to them. Isaiah is telling his fellow countrymen that they must repent of their sins. The first step in repentance or revival is to cease from doing wrong. Clean up your act. Give God real, honest, genuine worship.

Second, wash yourselves. King David prayed this same prayer centuries before when he asked God to create in him a clean heart, renew his spirit, restore the joy of his salvation, and deliver him from the guilt of bloodshed (Ps 51:10–14).

Third, he tells the people of Judah to **do right**. Seek justice. Simply put, obey God's Word.

Fourth, spend time in worship of God. ("Come, let us talk, reason together" 1:18.) This is the only command with a promised outcome. God calls people to come and spend time "with Me." He has promised that He will reveal how sins can be washed as white as snow.

The Calling in Worship (6:1–10)

At this point in Isaiah's journey, worship becomes a very personal experience—complete with the call and response. What follows are seven steps to transformational worship witnessed in the life of Isaiah:

First, Isaiah recognizes God as one sitting on a very high throne. God allows Isaiah to see His glory ("It was the Lord sitting on a very

high throne" 6:1–4). This one experience gave Isaiah enough power
to do the work of God for the rest of his life. Like Abraham, Jacob,
Moses, Joshua, Samuel, Deborah, and Gideon before, the prophet
was never the same after witnessing the sheer magnitude of God's
glory. He saw the holiness of God. God showed him the depth and
breadth of His wonders. Isaiah recognized God's sovereign rule. He
saw how God's glory fills the whole of earth. Isaiah marveled at how
the temple trembles when the sovereign voice of God speaks.

Second, Isaiah is struck with a spirit of conviction. "So I said:
'Woe *is* me, for I am undone!'" (6:5a NKJV). He perceives his own
sinfulness. His response is personal. He doesn't send a surrogate to
God. Rather, he personally seeks God with passion. He wants to
do something about his helpless condition—no matter the cost. He
instinctively knows the first step is repentance. A. W. Tozer wrote,

> What good is all our busy religion if God isn't in it? What good
> is it if we've lost majesty, reverence, worship—an awareness of
> the divine? What good is it if we've lost a sense of the Presence
> and the ability to retreat within our own hearts and meet God in
> the garden? If we've lost that, why build another church? Why
> make more converts to an effete Christianity? Why bring people
> to follow after a Savior so far off that He doesn't own them?
>
> We need to improve the quality of our Christianity, and we
> never will until we raise our concept of God back to that held
> by apostle, sage, prophet, saint and reformer. When we put God
> back where He belongs, we will instinctively and automatically
> move up again; the whole spiral of our religious direction will be
> upward.[4]

Third, we see Isaiah's profession of faith. Simply put, Isaiah
confesses his sin. "I am a man of unclean lips, and I dwell in the midst
of a people of unclean lips; for my eyes have seen the King, the LORD
of hosts" (Isa 6:5b NKJV). This prophet understood the depth of his
sin, and he understood the consequences of being in the company of

---

[4] A. W. Tozer, *The Knowledge of the Holy: The Attributes of God* (Lincoln, NE:
Back to the Bible Broadcast, 1971), 194–95.

sinners. He took a hard look at himself and in essence said, "God, I am not worthy to be in your presence, I'm a sinner" (my paraphrase). The philosopher Socrates said, "An unexamined life is not worth living." A. W. Tozer continues:

> If a common philosopher could think that, how much more we Christians ought to listen to the Holy Spirit when he says, "Examine yourself." An unexamined Christian lies like an unattended garden. Let your garden go unattended for a few months, and you will not have roses and tomatoes but weeds. An unexamined Christian life is like an unkempt house. Lock your house up as tight as you will and leave it long enough, and when you come back you will not believe the dirt that got in from somewhere. An unexamined Christian is like an untaught child. A child that is not taught will be a little savage. It takes examination, teaching, instruction, discipline, caring, tending, weeding and cultivating to keep the life right.[5]

Fourth, Isaiah seeks forgiveness and cleansing: "One of the heavenly creatures used a pair of tongs to take a hot coal from the altar. Then he flew to me with the hot coal in his hand. The creature touched my mouth with the hot coal and said, 'Look, your guilt is taken away, because this hot coal has touched your lips. Your sin is taken away'" (6:6–7 NCV). Once Isaiah confessed his need of forgiveness, God took over. The task of cleansing, purifying, and purging of sin was all God. So it is with you and me. God is the one responsible for the cleaning up portion. "For by grace you have been saved through faith, and that not of yourselves; it is the gift of God" (Eph 2:8–9 NKJV). We only need to confess our need and submit to His authority. He does the rest. Hallelujah!

Fifth, Isaiah answers the call. He hears God's voice, perceives the need, and recognizes a calling from God. "Also I heard the voice of the Lord, saying: 'Whom shall I send, and who will go for Us?'" (6:8 NKJV). God's call is not for the faint of heart. He did not tell Isaiah

---

[5] A. W. Tozer, comp. James L. Snyder, *Rut, Rot or Revival: The Condition of the Church* (Camp Hill, PA: Christian Publications, 1992), 43.

that the task, duty, or job would be easy. He did guarantee that the job ahead would be strategic:

> If you want to pray strategically, in a way which would please God, pray that God might raise up men who would see the beauty of the Lord our God and would begin to preach it and hold it out to people, instead of [just] offering peace of mind, deliverance from cigarettes, a better job and nicer cottage.[6]

God gave Isaiah the responsibility of proclaiming judgment and blessing, justice and righteousness, punishment and hope, devastation and salvation. No other prophet had ever been given such a daunting task. Isaiah's response?

Sixth, Isaiah answers God's call (6:8). Isaiah gives God total dedication and devotion. He makes a pledge to God. He consecrates his confession by responding, "Here am I! Send me. "

Seventh, Isaiah receives his commission and charge. Isaiah captures a sense of his task and immediately obeys. The job is not going to be easy, but Isaiah receives his instructions, accepts his duty, and serves the Lord with passion:

> Then the Lord said, "Go and tell this to the people: 'You will listen and listen, but you will not understand. You will look and look, but you will not learn.' Make the minds of these people dumb. Shut their ears. Cover their eyes. Otherwise, they might really understand what they see with their eyes and hear with their ears. They might really understand in their minds and come back to me and be healed." (6:9–10 NCV)

Time after time, we have seen that out of a heart of worship comes obedience. God enriches our worship as we obey His sweet, loving, tender voice. Foundational to worshipping God is obedience of God's Word.

God did not promise Isaiah that the task would be easy. To the contrary, He promised him that he would speak to a people who

---

[6] Tozer, *The Knowledge of the Holy*, 194–95.

would not listen. He did not promise Isaiah that there would be results—ever. He did guarantee him companionship, relationship, and a promise that "the Lord Himself will give you a sign: Behold, the virgin shall conceive and bear a Son, and shall call His name Immanuel" (7:14 NKJV).

Isaiah teaches us that worship of God is at the core of all we have in Christ. Worship is not determined by our faithfulness to the law. Our worship is evidenced or confirmed by our love for God.

Principles about Worship from This Chapter

What have we learned from Isaiah about transformational worship? We have learned the same lesson that the apostle Paul learned centuries later. It is when we worship Jesus that we become transformed worshippers:

> From this time on we do not think of anyone as the world does.
> In the past we thought of Christ as the world thinks, but we
> no longer think of him in that way. If anyone belongs to Christ,
> there is a new creation. The old things have gone; everything
> is made new! All this is from God. Through Christ, God made
> peace between us and himself, and God gave us the work of
> telling everyone about the peace we can have with him. God
> was in Christ, making peace between the world and himself.
> In Christ, God did not hold the world guilty of its sins. And he
> gave us this message of peace. So we have been sent to speak for
> Christ. It is as if God is calling to you through us. We speak for
> Christ when we beg you to be at peace with God. Christ had no
> sin, but God made him become sin so that in Christ we could
> become right with God. (2 Cor 5:16–21 NCV)

Here is the application from Isaiah and the apostle Paul. **First, obedience is still at the core of authentic, transformational worship.** To obey the Word of the Lord is better than anything. We demonstrate our love—our worship—of God best when we do what He tells us to do. When we obey His Word, our worship becomes transformational.

Second, when we see God—even in our worship—we are always made aware of our own sin. Once we see sin as compared to our awesome Lord, the first act of worship is to seek forgiveness and restoration with God. It is then that we recognize Him as the Lord of lords and King of kings. As we repent, God transforms us and makes us new.

Third, God is most glorified when He sees His work grow and develop in our lives. He gives comfort, peace, contentment, and direction for life. As we worship, He gives more of Himself to us. We experience His comfort, His peace, and His love in a powerful way. He gives us opportunity to walk with Him, talk with Him, trust Him, and declare His wonders to unbelievers around us. He transforms our daily walk.

Four, when God created us to worship, He carried out His plan for our lives—to know Him. He provided an avenue for communication with Him. He provided a way to make us better. He gave us hunger for completeness in Him. This is transformational worship.

Five, Jesus Christ is the focal point of all worship. This too is in God's plan. He is the focal point of redemption. He is the focal point of resurrection. He is the focal point of eternal life. He is the focal point for fellowship with God. He is the hope of the ages. He is the focal point of our worship. His plan for worship is based on how we embrace the truth that Jesus is the Lamb of God that takes away the sins of the world.

Transformational worship is individual. The point being made with our brief study of Jacob, Jonah, Ezekiel, Paul, Peter, and Isaiah is that transformation is deeply personal. It is something that must be experienced by each person as he or she worships the Lord. I cannot experience the transforming power of the Holy Spirit for anyone else. It is only a transformation that God can do in my life for me, individually.

This transformation can take place even in a crowd of people. While transformational worship is individual, it is also corporate. It doesn't have to be experienced alone. As we experience God's transformational power, we are able to worship more richly together.

I believe that is what happened in Acts 2. The Holy Spirit came upon each person individually, but the Spirit's presence and power impacted the entire group corporately. That is transformational worship. It is the power of God upon lives—individually and corporately.

Transformational worship takes time. Transformation is a ministry of the Holy Spirit and does not always take place in one worship service or one encounter with God. While our worship services need to be engaging, Christ honoring, and God exalting, the transformation that takes place during our worship only comes from a work of the Holy Spirit.

Renovation on this level takes time. Transformation only comes as we spend time in honest and heartfelt prayer. We simply must spend time with God. Transformational worship happens when we share our encounter with God with others. Transformational worship happens as we feed on His Word. In the process our transformation impacts those around us:

> The world is not transformed by relevant Christians, strategic Christians, visionary Christians, leadership-saavy Christians, wealthy Christians, attractive Christians, educated Christians, active Christians, or articulate Christians. These are all interesting qualities, and might be helpful on occasion—especially in building religious organizations and selling books. Ultimately, the world is transformed by sanctified Christians through whom the life of Jesus becomes a mystifying manifestation. People changed by Jesus cannot help but change the world.[7]

Discussion Questions

1. Explain the concept of transformation as it relates to being "changed" by God. How does this relate to worship and the Great Commission?

---

[7] Daniel Henderson, *Transforming Prayer* (Minneapolis: Bethany House, 2011), 36.

2. In reference to Isaiah's approach to spiritual transformation, explain the "criteria for worship."

3. Again, in reference to Isaiah's approach to spiritual transformation, fully discuss the "calling in worship." Include all seven points!

4. Why is transformational worship essential to fully understanding the Great Commission?

5. What concept is the heart of transformational worship? Explain.

CHAPTER 6

Great Commission Worship Is Relational (Part 1)

God never changes moods or cools off in His affections or loses enthusiasm. His attitude towards sin is now the same as it was when He drove out the sinful man from the eastward garden, and His attitude toward the sinner the same as when He stretched forth His hands and cried, "Come unto me, all ye that labour and are heavy laden, and I will give you rest."

A. W. Tozer[1]

In our last chapter, we learned that Great Commission worship is transformational. We are in the process of being changed. God uses this dynamic relationship in worship to change us from old to new, dead to living, and corruptible to incorruptible. As we worship, God changes the way we think, how we live, and who we love. Great Commission worship is also relational.

---

[1] A. W. Tozer, cited in Robert Morgan, ed., *Stories, Illustrations, and Quotes* (Nashville: Thomas Nelson, 2000), 357.

God made us to enjoy bright, vibrant, living relationships. He is the God of relationships. In fact, life is about relationships. The relationship designed by God for communion with His people is first an upward relationship—one that reflects our worship of God and the personal relationship we have with Him.

The Quest for Upward Relationship

Relational worship is based on friendship, affinity, and a bond with God. The quest for an upward relationship is actually the pursuit of upward worship. Our worship is the sum of all relationships we have with God. He is the one who initiates this relationship.

Consider this: God fashioned man out of dust for this one purpose—to worship Him. He carved from the rib of man, a woman to worship Him. God gave Adam and Eve a unique glimpse of perfect worship. They received great pleasure from worshipping Him. They had free will and minds capable of making right choices as they found total fulfillment in being with God.[2]

Worship in the garden of Eden was perfect worship. Imagine what perfect worship looks and feels like: closing your eyes each night after a very busy day in the arms of God, and waking in the morning after complete, peaceful, and uninterrupted rest. In this place it was natural to love God—free from any agenda or selfish motive. The couple were able to walk with God in the cool of the evening, knowing in their hearts that God was near and true. Surely this is what the relationship was like for Adam and Eve in Genesis 2—a state of perfect worship.

Even after the fall, God is still in the business of building relationships. He wants to have a relationship with us that is holy and perfect. While we cannot totally experience perfect worship until we arrive in heaven, we can enjoy His presence, thrill at His wonder, and love Him supremely. In return, God nurtures us, speaks peace to us, and cares for us—just as He did with Adam and Eve. Herein is the principle: our

---

[2] This is consistent with Charles C. Ryrie, *Basic Theology* (Wheaton, IL: Victor, 1988; reprint, Chicago: Moody, 1999), 202.

worship *of* God is the foundation of our relationship *with* God. Our relationship *with* God is in direct proportion to our worship *of* Him.

This relationship with God, however, focuses entirely on one person—God Himself. Yet, God focuses on meeting us at the point of our greatest need. This principle is most clearly seen in our worship of God. The more God reveals Himself to us, the more we love Him. The more we love Him, the more we learn about Him. The more we learn to know Him, the more we worship Him. The more we worship Him, the stronger our relationship grows with Him. This relationship of worship includes three essential elements: a desire for God, a dependence on God, and a delight in God.

Desire for God

The purpose for the creation of the world and the revelation of Jesus both center in God's plan for intimate relationship with those He created. In order to make this happen, God strategically places in the heart of each person an impulse or *desire* to seek, know, comprehend, value, pursue, and love Him. A. W. Tozer supports this notion by saying, "We pursue God because, and only because, he has first put an urge within us that spurs us to the pursuit."[3] Because God has placed this impulse in our hearts, we can know Him and enjoy a relationship with Him that is personal and intentional. Our sin blocks the power to know Him. The moment we establish a relationship with God, however, the inner desire to know, love, worship, and serve Him springs to life. Now a new encounter with the living God of the universe begins to take shape. At the origin of this relationship sparks an incredible pursuit to know God. This relationship impacts our will, ability to reason, consciousness, and motives:

> God is a person, and in the deep of his mighty nature he thinks, wills, enjoys, feels, loves, desires and suffers as any other person may. In making himself known to us he stays by the familiar

---

[3] A. W. Tozer, *Pursuit of God* (Harrisburg, PA: Christian, 1946; repr., Camp Hill, PA: Wingspread, 2006), 11.

pattern of personality. He communicates with us through the avenues of our minds, our wills, and our emotions. The continuous and unembarrassed interchange of love and thought between God and the soul of the redeemed man is the throbbing heart of New Testament religion.[4]

Desire for God is the fuel that builds our relationship with Him. God made us for relationship, friendship, communion, camaraderie, and companionship. Relationship with God and with others matures as we spend time with God together. The desire to experience God emerges as a reaction to our own personal instincts. We will naturally respond to being loved by showing love. God loves us. We naturally want to show love to Him in response.

The desire *for* God is one of the defining realities of worship. God wants to be known on an intimate basis. He aspires to enjoy an open and honest relationship with you and me. It is *this* desire for God that sets us apart from all other living creatures. Leonard Sweet defines this desire as a "quest" that results in a God-Life relationship:

> Part of the uniqueness of humanity, beings created in the image of God, is our instinct to seek and to enjoy the pleasures of seeking. It is born in us to dare, to desire, and to delight in the Quest. Questing-made-possible is who we are. Some say it's our sole advantage as a species. But the Quest is not a set of questions. The Quest is the mystery of getting lost in the God-Life relationship.[5]

Through the centuries, men and women have sought to know God in a relationship that transcends time and understanding. Abraham sought God and worshipped as he looked to the Promised Land. Moses sought the Lord and saw God's glory. King David sought God with a deep sense of spiritual desire, and the

---

[4] Ibid., 13.

[5] Leonard Sweet, *Out of the Question . . . into the Mystery* (Colorado Springs, CO: WaterBrook, 2004), 10. The premise of Sweet's book is that worship is built on a God-Life relationship. He contends that faith itself is a relationship. He supports this thesis by investigating the truth of relationships with God, God's story, other people of faith, those outside of faith, God's creation, the spiritual world, and other things.

Lord gave him songs in the night. While in the wilderness David proclaimed, "O God, you are my God, I seek you, my soul thirsts for you; my flesh faints for you, as in a dry and weary land where there is no water" (Ps 63:1 NRSV). The Hebrews sang, "As a deer longs for flowing streams, so my soul longs for you, O God" (Ps 42:1 NRSV). The Samaritan woman encountered Jesus in John 4 and confessed her desire to understand the wonders of the coming Messiah. The apostle Paul confessed that the burning desire of his heart was to "know Him and the power of His resurrection, and the fellowship of His sufferings" (Phil 3:10).

Dependence on God

It may not be politically correct to say, but "we are dependent upon God for everything." Everything. He is our counselor, companion, care-giver, and guardian. God is committed to building a loving, meaningful, grace-filled relationship with you and me.

God is Jehovah-Jireh—our provider. He places food on our tables and cares for our every physical, emotional, and spiritual needs. His Word says the righteous will *not* go hungry or go begging bread (Prov 10:3; Pss 107:9; 146:6b). He gives us a home, a place to sleep, and shelter from the elements of life. In short, we serve a God who meets our every need. He provides for our every care and worry. The apostle writes, "Give your worries to him because he cares about you."[6] He desires to meet every physical, emotional, and spiritual need in our lives.

God is our protection. The psalmist understood this protection principle as he sought God during a time of imminent danger:

Who is God? Only the Lord.
Who is the Rock? Only our God.
God is my protection.

---

[6] 1 Pet 5:7: "Cast all your anxiety on him because he cares for you" (NIV). "Give all your worries to him because he cares about you" (NCV). "Casting all your care upon him; because he careth for you" (KJV).

He makes my way free from fault.
He makes me like a deer that does not stumble;
He helps me stand on the steep mountains.
You protect me with your saving shield.
You Support me with your right hand.
You have stooped to make me great.
You give me a better way to live,
so I live as you want me to.
You gave me strength in battle.
The Lord lives!
May my Rock be praised.
So I will praise you, LORD, among the nations.
I will sing praises to your name. (Ps 18:31–36,39,46,49 NCV)

God sends angels to protect you and me from harm and minister to our various needs.[7] He protects us from those who would say evil and seek to damage our reputations, integrity, and character. He protects us spiritually, emotionally, and physically. Remember, "Our struggle is not against flesh and blood, but against the rulers, against the authorities, against the powers of this dark world and against the spiritual forces of evil in the heavenly realms" (Eph 6:12 NIV). Sometimes, God even protects us from seeing, hearing, and experiencing the peril and unsafe environment around us.

God grants to us His peace. I've already mentioned how God provides freedom from worry, but He also gives peace of heart. This has to do with a state of mental and emotional calm. God settles our anxious spirit.

The apostle Paul reminds us to "let the peace of God rule in your hearts, to which also you were called" (Col 3:15 NKJV). When we live in God's peace, there is no apprehension, distress, worry, dread, panic, fright, or trepidation. He guards and protects our hearts and keeps us close to His side. God protects us as we fellowship with Him. We can rest in the confidence that we are free from guilt, conflict, disagreement, war, anger, envy, covetousness, resentfulness, and even

---

[7] Gen 21:17–20; 1 Kgs 19:5–7; 2 Kgs 6:13–17; Pss 34:7; 91:11; Dan 6:20–23; Matt 1:20–21; Luke 1:11–20; Acts 7:52–53; 8:26; Heb 1:14.

a jealous spirit. God gives peace. He settles our spirit. We are at peace with God and with one another. Our egos stay in check. God meets every hunger of our soul and in the process grants total, unreserved peace, calm, and quietness of heart.

Several years ago, a friend invited me to go deep-sea fishing with his sons off the coast of Pensacola, Florida. We left port at the break of day just as the sun was peeking its head above the eastern horizon. The waters were totally calm. There was no wind. It was as if I were captured in a moment in time. The earth seemed rested and confident. As the boat moved through the water all creation seemed to say, "God is in control." Porpoises played in the calm of the morning. A huge sea turtle swam gracefully along the top of the water. All was at rest. One could sense the peace of God.

God wants to give you peace. He wants to replace the tempestuous inclination in your heart to feed your ego, strut your stuff, mark your territory, and prove your authority with a deeper experience of His grace and peace. He desires to calm your fear of failure with His gentle spirit. God desires to nurture His relationship with you so that self-confidence, poise, self-assurance, self-belief, and faith come as gifts from His hand.

God has a plan for your life. All that He has planned for us is based on the relationship we maintain with Him. As we wait for His plan to unfold before us, He works out what is best for our lives. He reveals something of His purpose for us. Leonard Sweet captures this truth through these fascinating words:

> We need the courage of our relationships—especially the
> courage of a right relationship with the Creator, the creation, and
> our fellow creatures. God is a mystery, not a master's thesis. We
> have much to learn about the truth of God that is revealed only
> through relationship.[8]

---

[8] Sweet, *Out of the Question*, 3, 10.

Delight in God

The third element in building this relationship with our loving God involves delight. There is a difference between desire and delight. Desire implies a hunger for God—a pursuit after Him, to know Him. Delight, on the other hand, describes our reaction to this relationship with Him.

I graduated from the University of Oklahoma. It is no secret that over the decades the university has amassed a huge, loyal following totally dedicated to Oklahoma Sooner football. I'm guilty. I love OU football. A loyal OU football fan desires to know more about each new player, new strategies for winning games, the latest college rankings, important statistics, and even the comings and goings of the coaching staff. One might say that a loyal OU Sooner is obsessed with a desire to know more about OU football.

But, their desire to know more about OU football fades when compared to the delight they experience when the team wins a championship, tournament, or bowl game. Desire turns into delight as the fans witness and enjoy all that the team can do.

Delight implies great joy and pleasure, happiness, glee, and enjoyment. John Piper says, "God is most glorified in us when we are most satisfied in Him."[9] The psalmist reminds us to "delight yourself in the LORD, and he will give you the desires of your heart" (Ps 37:4 NIV). The relationship with God is something we experience and enjoy. In the presence of God is fullness of joy, and at His right hand are pleasures forever (see Ps 16:11). There is exceeding joy in knowing God (see Ps 43:4). The great psalmist of Israel declares, "How sweet are Your words to my taste! Yes, sweeter than honey to my mouth!" (Ps 119:103 NKJV). The truth of God's message in 1 John is for our "joy to be full" (1 John 1:4). The apostle Paul encourages the brethren under the siege of persecution to "rejoice in the Lord always" (Phil 4:4 NKJV).

Herein is the secret of this relationship with God. We find our joy in Him. God responds by giving us more joy. Our response becomes

---

[9] John Piper, *Desiring God* (Portland, OR: Multnomah, 1986), 50.

an outgrowth of that which God is doing in our hearts. And, as C. S. Lewis exclaims, "all enjoyment spontaneously overflows into praise."[10]

We delight in God because He created us to enjoy Him. The hidden secret in building a relationship with God is confirmed as we learn and believe that God formed and created us for His glory and calls us by name. The Westminster Catechism asserts that "the chief end of man is to glorify God and enjoy him forever." This is the secret of perfect worship. We establish our relationship with God as we love Him, give our hearts to Him, enjoy His presence, thrill at the wonder of His mighty acts, and spontaneously explode with expressions of praise to Him:

> To love God does not mean to meet His needs, but rather to delight in Him and to be captivated by His glorious power and grace, and to value Him above all other things on earth. All the rest of the commandments are the kinds of things that we will do from our hearts, if our hearts are truly delighted with and resting in the glory of God's grace.[11]

Principles about Great Commission Worship from This Chapter

We have learned that Great Commission worship is relational. It is first an **Upward Relationship.**

1. **God delights in our relationship *with* Him.** God is most pleased when we are satisfied in Him. He is our song in the morning and our strength at night. Trust Him and He will fulfill your deepest desires.

2. **God nurtures our relationship as we worship Him.** God is vitally interested in seeing us establish a relationship as a daily companionship with Him as the living Lord of the universe. He desires that this relationship with Him be active, vibrant, energetic, and a true holy friendship. God wants to walk with us. He does not

---

[10] C. S. Lewis, *Reflections on the Psalms* (New York: Harcourt, Brace, Jovanovich, 1958), 94–95.

[11] Piper, *Desiring God*, 259.

walk or run ahead of us. He walks *with* us. As we seek to know Him, He nurtures this relationship—personally, individually, and lovingly.

3. **God reveals Himself through this loving relationship.** This principle is at the heart of His motive in establishing a relationship with you and me. God wants to reveal more of Himself so that we will enjoy worshipping Him. As we worship, He reveals more of His wonder, glory, and majesty. As we grow and mature in our understanding of God, that relationship grows and develops. As we enjoy being with Him, God grants to us the opportunity to rest in His peace and assurance. As we work for Him, serve Him, and "go into all the world" for Him, He promises His presence and His favor.

4. **You can establish a personal relationship with God, right now.** Yes, you can establish a personal relationship with God right where you are. How does this happen, you might ask? How does one become a worshipper of God?

First, realize that you are a sinner. God's Word teaches us that all of us are sinners. It is because of our sin that all people from every generation experience death (see Rom 6:23). Even though we are sinners, God loves us so much that He sent His Son to live on this earth, die on a cross, and rise victorious over death—so that we could become worshippers (see Rom 5:8–9).

Second, ask Jesus to forgive you of your sins. The next step in becoming a worshipper of God involves repentance. This is recognizing the wrong you have done and being sorry about it. It involves feeling regret about sin or past actions and changing your ways or habits. It involves living for God instead of self. This is transformational worship in action.

Third, accept Christ as your savior. God sent Jesus Christ into this world for the sole purpose of providing a way for you and me to have a living, loving relationship with God. The Bible teaches that if we confess with our lips that Jesus is Lord and believe in our hearts that God raised Him from the dead, we can become genuine worshippers of God. When we believe in our hearts, God removes all the sin from our lives and we stand before Him as justified by faith. We use our mouths to say we believe. By God's grace, we become worshippers and the relationship that we were made to enjoy with God begins (see Rom 10:9–10).

God secures this relationship with Him in heaven through the shed blood of Jesus Christ. The relationship God wants to share with you is a companionship that endures forever. It is an eternal relationship.

While Great Commission worship is relational, it is also a horizontal relationship. It has everything to do with our relationships with other people. In our next chapter, we will learn about horizontal relationships and how they apply to our worship.

Discussion Questions

1. Discuss what it means to have a "desire" for God. How does that apply to you?

2. Discuss what it means to have a "dependence" on God. How does that apply to you?

3. Discuss what it means to "delight" in God. How does that apply to you?

4. Where do you struggle the most in your vertical relationship with God? Trust? Being faithful?

5. Wherever you are, find a quiet place and spend at least five minutes delighting in God. Take a pencil and a piece of paper and write a note to God expressing your love and commitment.

CHAPTER 7

Great Commission Worship Is Relational (Part 2)

Christianity doesn't get more basic. . . . It is seeing value in, and loving and caring for, and reaching out to, and spending time with "the least of these."

Chuck Swindoll[1]

We learned in our last chapter that Great Commission worship is relational. Our focus in that study was on the relationship we have with God. This relationship is designed by God—reflecting our worship of God and the personal relationship we have with Him. We learned that God made us to enjoy bright, vibrant, living relationships. Everything we do reflects the relationships we have with God, our family, our fellow workers, and our friends.

The Quest for Horizontal Worship

It seems fairly natural that our worship would be upward to God, but Great Commission worship does not stop there. It involves

---

[1] Charles R. Swindoll, *Compassion* (Waco, TX: Word Books, 1984), 60.

application. "How does my upward worship impact other people in my life?"

When discussing horizontal relationships, I am specifically talking about the application of upward worship to our daily life. Our horizontal relationships are a reflection of the depth, duration, and quality of our upward worship of God and God alone.

Horizontal relationships are vitally important to our spiritual development. The apostle Paul addresses the whole idea of the worship of God as it directly applies to life's relational components. Check out Rom 12:9–15:9 and Col 3:17–20. The issues associated with relationships are grouped into four areas: (1) relationships with our families; (2) relationships with all people—believers and unbelievers; (3) relationships with those in authority; and (4) business relationships.

First, let's consider **the relationships with our family**. Two strategic areas are dealt with when the New Testament deals with family relationships. The first involves our attitude or spirit. In Ephesians, Colossians, and Romans, we are given instructions to "always [give] thanks to God the Father for everything, in the name of our Lord Jesus Christ" (Eph 5:20 NIV). Colossians 3:17 broadens the instruction to include our deeds: "and whatever you do, whether in word or deed, do it all in the name of the Lord Jesus, giving thanks to God the Father through him" (Col 3:17 NIV). The second strategic area for building relationships with our families has to do with our deeds—how we treat one another. Look at this list:

- "Submit to one another out of reverence for Christ" (Eph 5:21 NIV).
- "Wives, submit yourselves to your own husbands as to the Lord" (Eph 5:22 NKJV).
- "Now as the church submits to Christ, so also wives should submit to their husbands in everything" (Eph 5:24 NIV).
- "Wives, submit to your husbands, as is fitting in the Lord" (Col 3:18 NIV).
- "Husbands, love your wives, just as Christ loved the church and gave himself up for her" (Eph 5:25 NIV).

- "In this same way, husbands ought to love their wives as their own bodies. He who loves his wife loves himself" (Eph 5:28 NIV).
- "Each one of you also must love his wife as he loves himself, and the wife must respect her husband" (Eph 5:33 NIV).
- "Husbands, love your wives and do not be harsh with them" (Col 3:19 NIV).
- "Children, obey your parents in everything, for this pleases the Lord" (Col 3:20 NIV).
- "Fathers, do not embitter your children, or they will become discouraged" (Col 3:21 NIV).

Great Commission worshippers must nurture their family relationships. They need to manage their own families so well that others will see how they live and agree that their family is worthy of full respect (1 Tim 3:4). The general consensus in New Testament teaching is that "if anyone does not know how to manage his own family, how can he take care of God's church?" (1 Tim 3:5 NIV).

Second, consider the **relationships with other people—believer and unbeliever alike**.

Great Commission worship is lifestyle worship in action. It is a 24-hour, seven-days-a-week commitment. If we have been formed or shaped by Great Commission worship and our hearts have been truly transformed by the power of the Holy Spirit, then everything we are and do in life should reflect our love for God and the people He has created.

Our daily actions toward all people should reflect an understanding of and commitment to lifestyle worship-evangelism. Our lifestyle worship-evangelism is not demonstrated by the number of programs at our church, the worship concerts we host for our fellowship of friends, or the scores of block parties and evangelism efforts we have in any given period of time. As important as those things might be in the life and body of the church or in building the kingdom of God, lifestyle worship-evangelism is best demonstrated in how we react to, treat, manage, and reach out to people.

Relationships with believers. We've already seen how the apostle Paul reminds us to present our bodies as a living sacrifice to the Lord in worship (Rom 12:1–2). Romans 12:3–15:9 shows us how to practice worship in our daily living. Paul says, "Be devoted to one another in brotherly love. Honor one another above yourselves" (Rom 12:10 NIV).

For the believer, living a lifestyle of worship begins with how well we love and respect our brothers and sisters in Christ. It is evidenced by our ability to treat everyone fairly.

Devotion to one another and honoring others above ourselves is so contrary to our twenty-first-century postmodern, humanistic, secularized culture and concepts of living. We live in a culture that is driven by self-centeredness in every area of life. High school and college students look to celebrities and dream of the day they can become famous. In many cases, they are driven by the desire to achieve and will often sacrifice everything (including their closest relationships) for a moment of pleasure brought by the applause of a crowd or approval of an adoring fan base. Yet, the practical application of this one principle, devotion to one another, is at the core of building relationships and unity between believers (Rom 15:9). If practiced on a regular basis, it will revolutionize our worship and evangelism endeavors. It is our devotion, loyalty, fidelity, dedication, and commitment to each other that makes for successful team building. Devotion to one another provides opportunity for us to be blessed when others succeed. Our joy is found when giving others opportunity to serve. We find our most fulfilling moments in seeing others become all that God has intended for them to be—reaching their goals, growing in grace, and developing their own skills for ministry.

In recent years, I've been privileged to take choir and instrumental worship teams to visit and work among the Russian-German churches in Germany. Many of the more than 2,600 churches in and around Germany were started as church plants during the days following freedom from communism. Beginning in 1989, entire families once held in oppression by evil Communist dictators and leaders of the former Soviet Union were given permission to move back to their home lands in Germany and Western Europe. Over a ten-year period, more than 14 million believers settled in the western parts of Europe and select cities in the United States. As they moved west, they brought their work ethic, culture, churches, and way of life—especially to Germany.

In Germany, Mennonite and Baptist families usually settled near some type of industrial center. As they began to dwell in these neighborhoods, build houses, populate schools, and most importantly, provide much needed work for the German economy, they established communities with strong family traditions and a deeply committed love and worship of God. These men and women possessed an impeccable character and a work ethic that enabled them to rise through the ranks in their respective jobs and quickly took on significant leadership roles.

In addition to maintaining a great testimony in their places of work, these brothers and sisters are keenly devoted to one another. They help each other build homes and establish churches. When there is sickness or death in one of their church families, the entire fellowship responds with love and personal care. Today, there are more than 2 million of these stalwart, determined, well-educated, and dedicated believers leading a resurgence of evangelical theology in Germany. They are devoted to each other in love, and their unquestionable relationships serve as examples of Great Commission worship.

Beyond devotion to a commitment to rejoice when others succeed, according to Paul's admonishment in Romans, we are also to "rejoice with those who rejoice; mourn with those who mourn" (Rom 12:15 NIV). I've often heard that it is easy to mourn with people when things are really tough. We are quick to put our arms around our brothers and sisters at the loss of a job, disappointing bankruptcy, struggle with a career, health problem, or even the death of a loved one. However, it is often a totally different set of reactions when our brothers in Christ enjoy the favor of the Lord, experience huge successes in their jobs, or get opportunities that we really want for ourselves. Most of us give in to our carnal flesh and begin to feel jealous or a tinge of resentment. This is especially true when those same favors, successes, and opportunities are not coming our way. Ironically, the Bible does not provide opportunity for us to choose which best fits our preference—rejoicing or mourning. Great Commission Worshippers are faithfully to rejoice with those who rejoice and mourn with those who mourn.

How do our lives demonstrate to those around us that we are worshippers? It begins with our love for others. It must be sincere (Rom 12:9). Our actions are the fruit of our worship with God. God expects no less. While we are to hate evil and cling to what is good (Rom 12:9), hating evil does not mean we demonstrate disregard or hatred for the person doing evil. Rather, we are to reach out to them, love them, and seek to build relationships with them, too.

Relationships with unbelievers. The issue of how we deal with unbelievers is another area of consideration when making application of worship to lifestyle worship-evangelism. Obviously, we are to live in harmony with one another (Rom 12:16). This statement can apply to believer and unbeliever alike. This is what genuine worshippers of God do.

Some years ago, I had the opportunity to teach at the University of Oklahoma School of Music. Granted, OU is a secular institution in every sense of the word. The school mission does not include the teaching and training of worshippers in the evangelical tradition. They do not teach evangelism or the biblical theology of building relationships. However, I found during my four years in postgraduate studies that the working relationship among those in the School of Music was professional on every level. I don't recall ever hearing a cross or unkind word spoken during my tenure there. The teachers, graduate assistants, staff, and graduate students were helpful, kind, and gracious. I'm certain that on occasion there were some very frank and honest discussions and disagreements about issues. Publicly, there was a professional persona that made for a pleasant work environment, enjoyable learning experience, and engaging platform for building relationships. If a secular institution can demonstrate this kind of pleasant behavior, all the more reason for those of us who name the name of Christ to place high on our agenda the practice of "getting along with one another."

Getting along with one another is one of the very best ways to give testimony that we are worshippers. Love your neighbors. That is what Jesus tells us, but do we really "love our neighbors"? The apostle Paul also reminds us that "love is the fulfillment of the law" (Rom 13:10 NIV). Those of us in ministry are sometimes really good about building relationships with our brothers and sisters in Christ—especially those that we partner with week after week—while never checking on the neighbor across the street who does not claim to know Jesus. We are quick to rally a group of young people to go down to the ghetto areas of town and participate in street evangelism, but we forget to offer our help to others across the street when they need food, transportation to the hospital, or counsel and care when going through times of stress and disappointment.

Just as when dealing with believers, Great Commission Worshippers are to practice hospitality with unbelievers (Rom 12:13). Our calling as Great Commission Worshippers is to treat everyone impartially—believer and unbeliever. That means we consider everyone with the same respect we would want for ourselves. We do not show favorites.

What about those who do us wrong? Are we often content to live in a cesspool of anger, resentment, and passive-aggressive behavior when we know that someone has done us wrong, misrepresented us, sought to undermine our ministry, or destroy our influence? Here is what the apostle Paul says in Romans (NIV) about relationships we have with those that persecute and do us evil.

1. "Be joyful in hope, patient in affliction, faithful in prayer" (v. 12).
2. "Bless those who persecute you; bless and do not curse" (v. 14).
3. "Do not repay anyone evil for evil" (v. 17). "Do not be overcome by evil, but overcome evil with good" (v. 21).
4. "Be careful to do what is right in the eyes of everybody" (v. 17).

5. "Live at peace with everyone" (v. 18).
6. "Do not take revenge, but leave room for God's wrath, for it is written: It is mine to avenge; I will repay" (v. 19).
7. "If your enemy is hungry, feed him; if he is thirsty, give him something to drink" (v. 20).

Third, consider the **relationships we have with those in authority over us**. Two commands deal with these relationships: submission to those in authority (Rom 13:1–5) and paying taxes (Rom 13:6). Why do you suppose the apostle Paul dealt with these two specific areas? There are obviously hundreds of other areas that could have been dealt with. I feel sure that one of the reasons the apostle Paul documents submission to those in authority and paying of taxes is because both areas involve our character, our personal testimony, and our reputations. Both areas reveal something about a person's integrity. The former is also a gauge of a person's humility. The latter is a barometer of an individual's honor.

We have an obligation to support and obey those who have authority over us. Some of us just don't like being told what to do, but obedience to those in authority over us is a reflection of our own humility, submission, and willingness to learn from other people.

Can you imagine how difficult it would have been to maintain a sweet, loving spirit as a slave? I'm certain that many slave-masters were totally inconsiderate, harsh, and demanding to those under their command. Yet, a slave's will was totally in submission to the master—like it or not. It was in this environment that the apostle Paul gave his Col 3:22 instruction for servants to "obey . . . earthly masters in everything; and do it, not only when their eye is on you and to win their favor, but with sincerity of heart and reverence for the Lord" (NIV).

This area of submission is critical for the Great Commission Worshipper. In many ways, how we react to those in authority shapes the way other people view us. Our submission to authority (and our reaction to those in authority) is an indicator of the depth and breadth of the relationship we have with God (our upward worship). How we react to those in authority impacts our public testimony.

Let's not fool ourselves into thinking that the testimony we have around other people is unimportant. People are watching how we act and react to the normal ebb and flow of life. In fact, unsaved people of all cultures largely base what they understand about Christ by observing the testimony we as worship-evangelists have at the workplace (or school), with our friends, and around our families:

- They watch when we lose our temper and say things that in our hearts we really don't mean and never intended to let slip through our lips.
- They watch when we don't always tell the truth.
- They watch when we are unkind to the sound guy in the back of the church, even though he is acting like a jerk and has settled into a life of bitterness and anger toward those he is called to serve.
- They watch when we are impatient with our wife and children and then smile like everything is okay when getting out of the car at church on Sunday morning.
- They watch when we take part in gossip and grumble about our boss or those in authority over us.
- They watch when we ignore directives from those designated to be our managers.
- They watch when we are rude to the cashier at the grocery store.
- They watch when we are envious of those that are successful.
- They watch and form their opinions about God when we refuse to follow through and obey those that have authority over us—even government authorities.

Not paying taxes when we know they should be paid is cheating, stealing, and robbing from the government. It is sin. We may not like how the government spends our money, but our biblical responsibility is to pay our taxes—all of them.

Ironically, most reading this book are not going to be guilty of dodging their annual tax bill. However, what about illegal downloading of iTunes from a friend's computer to avoid paying the downloading fees? Are we guilty of illegally copying songs onto CDR's for use in rehearsal and not once contacting any publisher, record company, or copyright broker about royalty payments? What about the DVD of the movie copied to your iPod for the purpose of showing it to a group of 75 at the New Year's eve party, knowing all along that the law clearly prohibits the use of most movies with large groups? Do we really think that others are not watching our careless behavior? Here is the way the apostle Paul judges the matter:

> This is also why you pay taxes, for the authorities are God's servants, who give their full time to governing. Give to everyone what you owe him: If you owe taxes, pay taxes; if revenue, then revenue; if respect, then respect; if honor, then honor. (Rom 13:6–7 NIV)

Charles Finney said it best: "A person who is dishonest in little things isn't really honest in anything."[2] I might add that a dishonest person, even a Great Commission Worshipper, is probably inconsistent in maintaining a daily time in worship of God. Robert Morgan tells about Allen C. Emery's father's integrity and value for honesty in all matters of life:

> Once [my dad] lost a pair of fine German binoculars. He collected insurance only to find the binoculars a year later. Immediately he sent a check to the company and received a letter back stating that this seldom occurred and that they were encouraged. It was a small thing, but children never forget examples lived before them.[3]

Fourth, let's consider our **business relationships**. Remember, as Great Commission Worshippers, our business dealings must be above reproach. Our business dealings need to be always above board and with unquestionable integrity. To reach this level in business requires a consistent commitment to faithfulness.

---

[2] Robert Morgan, *Preacher's Sourcebook of Creative Sermon Illustrations* (Nashville: Thomas Nelson, 2007), 442.

[3] Ibid., 445.

Faithful to Honesty

Surely, Great Commission Worshippers would never have a problem in this area. Not so fast. It is absolutely amazing that we sometimes pass off "stealing" as unintentional misappropriation of product
or distribution of material for public relation purposes. Frank Saeks
writes in a September 2, 1996, article in the *Wichita Business Journal*
that . . .

> . . . according to the U.S. Department of Commerce,
> approximately a third of all business failures each year can be
> traced to employee theft and other employee crime. While
> managers and owners would like to think their employees are
> all trustworthy and honest, large-scale anonymous surveys have
> shown almost half of employees admitted to stealing.[4]

Honesty is a reflection of our integrity and a gauge of our commitment to genuine worship.

Faithful to Resolve Debt

The apostle once again reminds us that we must not be controlled by
debt: "Let no debt remain outstanding, except the continuing debt
to love one another, for he who loves his fellowman has fulfilled the
law" (Rom 13:8 NIV).

I remember having a lunch meeting some years ago with a well-
known business person in Nashville. This person owns a company that
provides recording products (CDs, DVDs, cassettes, and printing) for
hundreds of producers, music publishing companies, artists, and music
distributors around the world. During the course of our conversation,
the owner lamented that it was easier to get money on time from
secular companies, musicians, and artists than from those who called
themselves Christians. Christian businesses, the owner explained,
are always late making payments and constantly in debt. Obviously,

---

[4] Ibid., 444.

certain Christian businesses and artists did not leave a very healthy impression on this proprietor.

Faithful in Our Work

The final area for the Great Commission Worshipper has to do with how well we deliver and perform the task for which we have been assigned. The apostle Paul reminds us that "whatever [we] do, work at it with all [our] heart[s], as working for the Lord, not for men, since you know that you will receive an inheritance from the Lord as a reward. It is the Lord Christ you are serving" (Col 3:23–24 NIV). This is the key and the place where our worship and daily living intersect. We are serving Christ, and our worship is demonstrated by the way we love the Lord with all our heart, soul, mind, and strength.

Principles about Great Commission Worship from This Chapter

Yes, we have learned in this chapter that Great Commission worship is relational. It is a *horizontal relationship* that has everything to do with our association, connection, affiliation, and rapport with others.

As we continue our study together, it is important for us to remember that God created us in His image for the sole purpose of worshipping and glorifying Him. In the words of A. W. Tozer, "If we do not honor this purpose, our lives will degenerate into shallow, selfish, humanistic pursuits."[5]

If we honor His purpose for our lives, we will find absolute joy, contentment of heart, rationale for serving, and focus in living. In our next chapter, we will learn how we put this worship relationship into action through our own missional worship.

---

[5] A. W. Tozer, *Men Who Met God*, comp. and ed. Gerald B. Smith (Camp Hill, PA: Wingspread, 2009), 23.

Discussion Questions

1. Remembering the "Five Great Priorities" from chapter 6, along with information pertaining to relationships provided in this chapter, which of those priorities is most difficult for you to keep in the proper order?

2. With this in mind, take an honest look at your "family" relationships. Where do you need to improve?

3. Take an honest look at your relationships with "believers" and "unbelievers." Where do you need to improve?

4. Take an honest look at your "work" relationships. Where do you need to improve?

5. Write out ten names of people from each of these relational categories mentioned in the chapter. Make a commitment to pray specifically for each person on your list for the next ten days. Ask God to give you strength to share Christ with each of these people. You could begin by sharing your story through celebrating God's wonders in your life!

CHAPTER 8

Great Commission Worship Is Missional

> *God's evangelistic strategy in a nutshell: He desires to build into you and me the beauty of his own character, and then put us on display.*
>
> Joseph Aldrich[1]

The concepts of living a missional life or creating a missional church have become popular "buzz" words over the last few years. According to Ed Stetzer in his book, *Planting Missional Churches*, the key to understanding this idea is to first realize that the age of "Christendom" is dead. He writes:

> "Christendom," that realm or time when Christianity was the assumed religion of the West, has come to an end. No longer is Christianity the "chaplain" to the broader culture. Until the last several years in the history of the United States, Christianity was thought to be the "American religion" even though it was

---

[1] Quoted in Robert Morgan, ed., *Stories, Illustrations, and Quotes* (Nashville: Thomas Nelson, 2000), 777.

not embraced by everyone or practiced with devotion that committed Christians would like. It was once perceived as part of America's ethos.[2]

I have to believe that one of the main issues causing this demise has been the compartmentalizing of essential teachings related to worship, evangelism, and the Great Commission. To me, the most revealing part of the statement above relates to the Christian life not being "practiced with devotion that committed Christians would like."[3]

This is why our expressions of worship must be missional. Just as Christendom is dead, so is obedience to the Great Commission if worship and evangelism are characterized as merely outward expressions of one's faith rather than part of one's spiritual DNA.

Stetzer strikes a difference between a church that is "mission-minded" versus being "missional." He explains:

> Don't confuse the terms mission-minded and missional. The first refers more to an attitude of caring about missions, particularly overseas. Missional means actually doing mission right where you are. Missional means adopting the posture of a missionary, learning and adapting to the culture around you while remaining biblically sound. Think of it this way: missional means being a missionary without ever leaving your zip code.[4]

He goes on further to explain that a missional church is called to go "on-mission" with Christ. This simply means "being intentional and deliberate about reaching others."[5] This does not mean, however, that being missional is about merely "putting more time into reaching out to the neighborhood."[6] Rather, "being missional begins with a profound conviction that we are invited to join in the mission of God

---

[2] Ed Stetzer, *Planting Missional Churches* (Nashville: B&H, 2006), 19.
[3] Ibid.
[4] Ibid.
[5] Ibid.
[6] John Bailey, "The Missional Church," in *Pursuing the Mission of God in Church Planting*, comp. John Bailey (Alpharetta, GA: North American Mission Board, 2006), 39.

and that the church does not exist for itself, but rather for the world around us whom God so desperately loves."[7]

What Is a Missional Worshipper?

If the above statements are true, then being missional can easily be described as daily living out an authentic and intentional life of worship that embodies the ministry passions of Christ. In short, it means becoming a sold-out Great Commission Worshipper.

Worship is a critical connection to becoming a missional Christian. In order to explain the connection, you have to understand the tension that exists between temporal and eternal adoration for God. John Piper addresses this tension by describing the difference between missions and worship. According to Piper:

> Missions is not the ultimate goal of the church. Worship is.
> Missions exists because worship doesn't. Worship is ultimate,
> not missions, because God is ultimate, not man. When this age
> is over, and the countless millions of the redeemed fall on their
> faces before the throne of God, missions will be no more. It is a
> temporary necessity. But worship abides forever.[8]

I wanted to include this quote because in my opinion it is often used out of context to diminish what it means to live out a missional existence, as if there were no connection between worship and evangelism. I have actually heard fellow ministers use this statement to rationalize their disobedience to the Great Commission. Somehow, they have convinced themselves that they are more spiritual if they pursue the eternal calling of worship to the exclusion of the immediate command to live missionally by sharing Christ and serving a lost world.

At the very least, this kind of thinking is illogical and completely unbiblical. How is it possible to passionately pursue the heartbeat of

---

[7] Ibid.

[8] John Piper, *Let the Nations Be Glad! The Supremacy of God in Missions* (Grand Rapids: Baker Academic, 1993), 11.

God through worship and knowingly disobey Him at the same time? Isn't obedience the core value of biblical worship? Because of their disobedience in the temporal area of evangelism, these misinformed ministers forfeit the very thing they say they are pursuing—authentic worship!

The people I am talking about may sing songs and lift their hands, but they never share the gospel with their neighbors. They are in love with worship, but they forget that a worshipping saint will always engage in evangelism. It is totally impossible for persons who truly worship in spirit and truth not to demonstrate the wonders of God in their life as missional beings.

In no way do I believe we should ignore the temporal call of God to be involved in the Great Commission. It is our call to worship! The immediate "necessity" for "missions" is to proclaim the gospel until the day when Christ returns and every true believer is ushered into God's presence in heaven. At that point, there will no longer be any need for evangelism and we will worship eternally. Until then, we must do as Christ commands and passionately embrace our missional calling to spread the gospel to the ends of the Earth.

According to Van Sanders, God's design for the mission of His people "is to be his instrument through which he creates one, called out, holy people for his glory and worship from all peoples of the world."[9] I believe one of the greatest ways to express true worship as the church is to passionately live every day as missional believers. As we will see in Scripture, this is the essence of what it means to be a Great Commission Worshipper!

A Missional Approach to Scripture

In order to become missional worshippers, we must learn to interpret the Bible in terms of what Christopher Wright calls the missional hermeneutic. He explains:

---

[9] Van Sanders, "The Mission of God and the Local Church," in *Pursuing the Mission of God in Church Planting*, 15–16.

A missional hermeneutic, then, is not content to simply call for obedience to the Great Commission (though it will assuredly include that as a matter of nonnegotiable importance), nor even to reflect on the missional implications of the Great Commandment. For behind both it will find [in the Bible] the great Communication—the revelation of the identity of God, of God's action in the world and God's saving purpose for all creation.[10]

Wright is arguing that as the revelation of God, the entire Bible should be viewed through the missional lenses of interpretation. As an Old Testament theologian, he was concerned that his students would get the false impression that only certain parts of Scripture are applicable when explaining the missionary/evangelistic endeavors of God throughout time. As he sees it, "the Bible renders to us the story of God's mission through God's people in their engagement with God's world for the sake of the whole of God's creation."[11]

This radically challenges our approach to interpreting the Bible as it relates to God's missional work in history. I have always believed that the Bible is a living book, authored by God, and sent to man as a means of His grace—holy communication. That has not changed. However, if the whole Bible (Old and New Testaments) is to be interpreted in light of God's redeeming activity throughout history, it then becomes God's missionary journal to man, explaining how He has *always* been active in mobilizing His children into missional endeavors.[12]

Make no mistake about it, from Genesis to Revelation, God has actively pursued fallen men and women first to be redeemed and then to join Him on mission as Great Commission Worshippers to proclaim eternal hope to a lost world. This mandate has never changed!

---

[10] C. J. H. Wright, *The Mission of God* (Downers Grove, IL: InterVarsity, 2006), 61–62.

[11] Ibid., 21–22.

[12] Alvin Reid, *Evangelism Handbook* (Nashville: B&H, 2009), 49.

Some Biblical Models

As mentioned back in chapter 3, Great Commission Worshippers are *missional* on two levels:

> 1. They desire to take the gospel to the nations. Great Commission Worshippers seek to make disciples of Jesus by compelling people to become worshippers of the Living Lord, by sharing faith, promoting His wonders, preaching the good news, and proclaiming the glory of God.
>
> 2. Great Commission Worshippers reach out to the needy, feed the hungry, care for the sick, embrace the marginalized, adopt orphans, love the widows, and accept the unwanted.

Great Commission Worshippers literally become the hands and feet of Christ to the world! They are driven by a passion for God and a deep love for others. They internalize the missional call of God with such conviction that it becomes their life's driving passion.

We see this lived out through God's people in nearly every book of the Bible. From the act of creation where God's intent was to establish a people who would glorify Him and live in a glorious relationship of worship and freedom to the prophetic words of Abraham in Genesis 22:8 (NASB), that "God will provide for Himself the lamb," it is obvious that God's intent has always been to involve His people in missional endeavors that would allow us to take worship to the nations!

Many of the greatest examples of this missional theme are found in the psalms.

Psalm 96:1–3,10–13

It is easy to see the missional call of God in the words of the psalmist:

> Oh, sing to the LORD a new song! Sing to the LORD, all the earth. Sing to the LORD, bless His name; Proclaim the good news of His salvation from day to day. Declare His glory among the nations,

His wonders among all peoples. For the LORD *is* great and greatly
to be praised; He *is* to be feared above all gods. (NKJV)

Note the use of active words like *proclaim* and *declare*. It is obvious
that the psalmist is intimately connected to the missional call of the
Father as He disperses His children to address the nations about His
redemption. In doing so, we are given a glimpse of how God means
for evangelism and worship to co-exist.

I fear that too often we are guilty of communicating the
"message" of the gospel without considering the One who deserves
our adoration for His amazing "wonders." Every time we proclaim
His "wonders" through our witness to the world, it is a supreme act
of missional worship and evangelism.

The psalmist agrees. Notice further the words and expressions he
uses in verses 10–13 (NKJV):

Say among the nations, "The LORD reigns; the world also is firmly
established, it shall not be moved; He shall judge the peoples
righteously." Let the heavens rejoice, and let the earth be glad; let
the sea roar, and all its fullness; let the field be joyful, and all that
is in it. Then all the trees of the woods will rejoice before the
LORD. For He is coming, for He is coming to judge the earth. He
shall judge the world with righteousness, and the peoples with
His truth.

Because of the "wonders" of God expressed through His people and
mirrored in His creation, the nations can rest in the security that "the
world is firmly established, it shall not be moved." As a result, "the
heavens rejoice," and the psalmist proclaims, "Let the earth be glad!"
All of this reveals the missional desires of God and points to the one
who "is coming to judge the earth and the peoples with His truth."

Psalm 67:1–7

Notice a similar message in Psalm 67:

God be merciful to us and bless us, and cause His face to shine
upon us, Selah, that Your way may be known on earth, Your

salvation among all nations. Let the peoples praise You, O
God; let all the peoples praise You. Oh, let the nations be glad
and sing for joy! For You shall judge the people righteously, and
govern the nations on earth. Selah. Let the peoples praise You, O
God; let all the peoples praise You. Then the earth shall yield her
increase; God, our own God, shall bless us. God shall bless us,
and all the ends of the earth shall fear Him. (NKJV)

The psalmist's proclamation, "That Your way may be known
on earth, Your salvation among all nations," is a missional mandate
revealing the heart of God for an unsaved world. At the same time,
the call to "let the peoples praise You, O God; . . . let the nations
be glad and sing for joy" reveals the close relationship between
proclaiming God's wonders in worship and His missional call to
redeem the nations.

The progression is obvious. God's ultimate desire has never
changed from the moment He spoke the world into existence. He
desires genuine worship from His people! In return, He desires that
His message of hope be spread to the nations. When this occurs, "the
earth shall yield her increase; God shall bless us, and all the ends of
the earth shall fear Him."

Psalm 108:1–6

Once again, the psalmist describes a familiar scenario representing
a missional God, proclaiming a missional message, being lived out
through missional worshippers. He states:

O God, my heart is steadfast; I will sing and give praise, even
with my glory. Awake, lute and harp! I will awaken the dawn.
I will praise You, O LORD, among the peoples, and I will sing
praises to You among the nations. For Your mercy is great above
the heavens, and Your truth *reaches* to the clouds. Be exalted, O
God, above the heavens, and Your glory above all the earth; that
Your beloved may be delivered, save with Your right hand, and
hear me. (NKJV)

The statement, "I will sing praises to You among the nations" represents the missional call of God's worshippers not to be shy in proclaiming His "wonders" to the world. The ultimate result is that God's children and the nations will be "delivered."

The New Testament boasts numerous examples of this missional theme.

John 4:7–26,39–42

The story of "the woman at the well" in John 4 is a perfect example of the missional lifestyle of Christ that uniquely combined elements from both worship and evangelism. As we explore this passage, let's first consider the initial contact of Jesus with the adulterous woman in verses 7–12 (NKJV):

> A woman of Samaria came to draw water. Jesus said to her, "Give Me a drink." For His disciples had gone away into the city to buy food. Then the woman of Samaria said to Him, "How is it that You, being a Jew, ask a drink from me, a Samaritan woman?" For Jews have no dealings with Samaritans. Jesus answered and said to her, "If you knew the gift of God, and who it is who says to you, 'Give Me a drink,' you would have asked Him, and He would have given you living water." The woman said to Him, "Sir, You have nothing to draw with, and the well is deep. Where then do You get that living water? Are You greater than our father Jacob, who gave us the well, and drank from it himself, as well as his sons and his livestock?"

As you read over this section of chapter 4 in John, the character and compassion of Christ are evident in the masterful ways in which He treats the "woman at the well." Take note of the small nuances that verify His missional commitment to reach out to the unloved and disregarded in culture.

First, consider that Jesus "intentionally" traveled through Samaria! While verse 4 states that "He needed to go through Samaria," the truth is that many Jews never would have considered such a detour as a viable option.

Rather, they would have chosen to spend precious time traveling "around" Samaria rather than to risk the possibility of mingling with the despised "half-breeds." Keep in mind that the Jews did not merely "dislike" the Samaritans. The Jews viewed the Samaritans as impure and not worthy of God's mercy or their attention! They "hated" the Samaritans with great venom and passion!

The actions of Christ, at the very least, should compel the church to "intentionally" engage with cultural Samaritans. As Jesus states in Matt 25:40 (NKJV), "Assuredly, I say to you, inasmuch as you did it to one of the least of these My brethren, you did it to Me." Missional worshippers are always concerned with the needs of hurting people—especially if they have been disenfranchised by society!

Second, Jesus speaks to the woman. Who would have thought that a simple statement like "give me a drink" would have such a profound meaning? Jesus saw this woman in a different light. To Him, she was much more than a social outcast. To the average Jewish male, she represented two things they despised most: a Samaritan and a woman! According to their tradition these two issues were raised in prayer by Jewish males on a regular basis as they would thank God that they were not a "Samaritan" and again that they were not a "woman"!

Jesus' words were intriguing and inviting as the woman responded, "How is it that you, being a Jew, ask me for a drink since I am a Samaritan woman?" From this point, two things are evident about the missional actions of Jesus. First, His words affirmed the woman's humanity and her value to God. It is here that Christ helps her come to the reality of who she really is to God as Father. Contrary to Jewish beliefs, this Samaritan woman mattered to God and was deserving of Christ's attention, mercy, and the opportunity for salvation!

Second, He obviously cared more about the woman's soul than His religious traditions.

Because of Jesus' missional DNA, He was willing to drink from the same container as a known adulterer/sinner.

Imagine that! Unlike many of us, Jesus was even willing to get Samaritan germs if it resulted in gaining confidence with the woman for the sake of evangelism. The story continues in John 4:13–26 where Jesus further engages the woman concerning her sin and His real identity. He does this by responding to her earlier question, "Where then do you get that living water?" Jesus answers:

> "Whoever drinks of this water will thirst again, but whoever drinks of the water that I shall give him will never thirst. But the water that I shall give him will become in him a fountain of water springing up into everlasting life."
>
> The woman said to Him, "Sir, give me this water, that I may not thirst, nor come here to draw." Jesus said to her, "Go, call your husband, and come here." The woman answered and said, "I have no husband." Jesus said to her, "You have well said, 'I have no husband,' for you have had five husbands, and the one whom you now have is not your husband; in that you spoke truly." The woman said to him, "Sir, I perceive that you are a prophet. Our fathers worshipped on this mountain, and you Jews say that in Jerusalem is the place where one ought to worship." Jesus said to her, "Woman, believe Me, the hour is coming when you will neither on this mountain, nor in Jerusalem, worship the Father. You worship what you do not know; we know what we worship, for salvation is of the Jews. But the hour is coming, and now is, when the true worshippers will worship the Father in spirit and truth; for the Father is seeking such to worship Him. God is Spirit, and those who worship Him must worship in spirit and truth." The woman said to him, "I know that Messiah is coming" (who is called Christ). "When He comes, He will tell us all things." Jesus said to her, "I who speak to you am He." (NKJV)

On the heels of Christ's statements, the woman responds in what appears to be an affirmative manner. She asks "Sir, give me this water, that I may not thirst, nor come here to draw."

Could this mean that the woman was ready to respond to Christ or could it mean that she was just being sarcastic and still doubted? In either case, Jesus was careful not to pick the spiritual fruit too early. Regardless of the woman's motivation, Jesus was intentional in His actions yet patient to carefully engage the woman in a dialogue that ultimately leads to the truth.

Jesus knew that the woman must be confronted with her sin before there could be a serious discussion relating to her need of salvation. Jesus does this in verses 15–18 when He addresses the issue of her five husbands. Jesus had already established a rapport with the woman before confronting the issue of her sin. Dealing with sin is always imperative and essential, but the critical issue is how one accomplishes the task. In a relational culture, most people will not receive the truth until they first see the truth demonstrated in other believers. Missional worshippers must be genuine and real!

Jesus calls for the woman to submit her life and "worship the Father in Spirit and truth." A proper understanding of worship always involves the issue of total submission and surrender to the Lordship of the Father.

Regardless of religious traditions and personal preferences, we should always be careful not to limit God's grace and mercy to a certain segment of society or culture. It also bears noting that Jesus uniquely combines evangelism and worship as a singular expression of His missional call.

The woman responded that she knew the Messiah was coming. Jesus affirmed His deity and the woman summoned the town to come and hear this man. She wondered if He could be the Christ.

Here is an adulterous Samaritan woman. She is an outcast in her own society, not to mention among the Jews. Yet, after meeting Jesus, she leaves her "water pot" (an obvious sign that a significant transition was occurring in her heart) and she immediately becomes a missional worshipper inviting the whole city to meet the Messiah!

While the woman's response is powerful and convicting, the saga does not end here. Note verses 39–42 (NKJV):

> And many of the Samaritans of that city believed in Him
> because of the word of the woman who testified, "He told me all
> that I ever did." So when the Samaritans had come to Him, they
> urged Him to stay with them; and He stayed there two days.
> And many more believed because of His own word. Then they

said to the woman, "Now we believe, not because of what you said, for we ourselves have heard Him and we know that this is indeed the Christ, the Savior of the world."

Many of the Samaritans of that city believed in Christ because of the word of the woman who testified about Him (v. 39). Obviously, this speaks to the imperative that the church must never stop testifying about the works of Christ. Just as He used the woman at the well, God can use us in a similar manner if we are willing to boldly proclaim His wonders to the nations.

There is an even greater concept at work—the principle of natural reproduction. Note that after Jesus chooses to invest Himself (discipleship) and stay with the Samaritans for two more days, the ultimate outcome is that the Samaritans grasp this salvation and eventually claim it as their own. "Now we believe, not because of what you (the woman) said, for we ourselves have heard Him and indeed we know that this is the Christ, the Savior of the world" (v. 42).

This should always be the missional progression of salvation. It begins by way of the Holy Spirit as an expression of authentic worship in the hearts of men and women who are then redeemed and immediately become reproducing worshippers. This is evidenced by the fact that many biblical scholars believe that the Samaritan revival initiated through Philip in Acts 8 was the natural progression that began with a poor adulterous woman who became a missional worshipper in John 4.

Acts 2

In Acts 2, the Church is born when the Holy Spirit is revealed in power at Pentecost. As a result, Peter preaches a message of repentance and 3,000 people respond in faith. Almost immediately, the new believers adopt a missional mind-set of community, worship, and lifestyle evangelism. Note what the Bible says in verses 42–47 (NKJV):

And they continued steadfastly in the apostles' doctrine and fellowship, in the breaking of bread, and in prayers. Then fear came upon every soul, and many wonders and signs were done through the apostles. Now all who believed were together, and had all things in common, and sold their possessions and goods, and divided them among all, as anyone had need. So continuing daily with one accord in the temple, and breaking bread from house to house, they ate their food with gladness and simplicity of heart, praising God and having favor with all the people. And the Lord added to the church daily those who were being saved.

Unlike today, they were not trying to "attract" people to a location to hear the gospel. They understood the power of incarnationally becoming the message of Christ by representing God in a spirit of humility, worship, and unity. Somehow, they understood that worship and evangelism are more than religious practices. Their lives of missional authenticity were undeniable and opened the door to proclaim the wonders of Christ to a people looking to escape the bondage of Jewish legalism.

A Few Concluding Thoughts

Our mission to carry the gospel to a lost and dying world is the intent of the Great Commission, but at the heart of the Great Commission is worship of Jesus. The Holy Spirit equips, fills, energizes, and empowers worshippers to declare the wonders of God to the heathen.

Therefore, worship is missional! When God's people truly fall in love with Christ, they cannot be silent about His grace and mercy. Once the woman at the well understood the true identity of Jesus, she was compelled to worship Him in total obedience by proclaiming His message to her whole town. Look what happened! We must go and do the same!

Discussion Questions

1. What does it mean to live a "missional" life?

2. Explain the difference between being "mission-minded" and being "missional."

3. According to the author, how should the statement, "Missions exists because worship doesn't" be explained. Should evangelism be minimalized?

4. Explain what it means to apply a "missional" interpretation to Scripture?

5. What does it mean to celebrate God's "wonders"? How does this idea apply to becoming a missional worshipper?

CHAPTER 9

Great Commission Worship Is Reproducible . . .

Defining the Great Commission Worshipper (Part 1)

God places high value on holiness, reverence, and worship. He approved neither idol worship nor idle worship but ideal worship in Spirit and Truth.

Vance Havner[1]

In the book *Evangelism Is,* Dave Earley explains that evangelism is designed to be a reproducible lifestyle of worship for every Christian believer. He uses the incarnational picture of Christ as the example to be followed.

> In John 1:14, we read: "And the Word [Jesus, *logos*, message] became flesh and dwelt among us, and we beheld His glory, the glory as of the only begotten of the Father, full of grace and truth." The Greek term for "flesh" (*sarx*) is used when referring

---

[1] Vance Havner, *Don't Miss Your Miracle* (Grand Rapids, MI: Baker, 1984), 57.

to "flesh, muscles, tissue and the like." The implication is that Jesus, who was born physically, was a human being through and through. The word *incarnation* is taken from the Greek *in carne* or, literally, "in the flesh." "Dwelt," used in John 1:14, is an Aramaic term that could be translated "pitching one's tent." Linking the two ideas together, we see that Jesus did not merely shout the good news at us from heaven. No, He literally became one of us and "pitched the tent" of His life among us so He could get the message of God to us in a manner that was "full of grace and truth."[2]

You might be thinking that this is great information, but what does Jesus' incarnation have to do with developing a Great Commission Worshipper? It all depends on how one interprets the concept of biblical discipleship as it relates to becoming a reproducing worshipper.

Unfortunately, the process of discipleship has consistently been misinterpreted and misapplied in most Christian circles. Rather than creating "incarnational" warriors who feel compelled to reproduce by joining Christ on mission and "pitching their tent" among the unsaved, contemporary discipleship is often limited to merely attending weekly classes through the church or meeting in small groups with little or no expectation of becoming "Christ in flesh" to the world.

This type of anemic discipleship that does not reproduce is always detrimental to the Great Commission. Before going further, let's examine some common misunderstandings falsely attributed to biblical discipleship that hinder the spirit of reproduction.

Hindrances to Becoming Great Commission Worshippers

The Challenge of Education vs. Mobilization

The common belief among most Christians (even church leaders) is that a person must achieve a high level of biblical and practical knowledge before he can become a reproducing follower of Christ.

---

[2] Dave Earley and David Wheeler, *Evangelism Is* (Nashville: B&H, 2010), 184.

I hear this type of appraisal every semester with my undergraduate and graduate students at Liberty University.

While many of the students have been born again for several years, they continue to drink from the fountain of misinterpretation when it comes to feeling underprepared to join Christ on mission as a reproducing disciple. This feeling is exacerbated by the fact that through the evangelism classes, Liberty students are required to share their faith with someone during the semester and write a brief report about their experience. Over all, the main excuse for not sharing is a fear of rejection and a false belief that without experience and knowledge the witness cannot be effective.

Nothing could be further from the truth. Consider the approach that Christ used with His disciples in Matt 10:16–20 (NKJV):

> "Behold, I send you out as sheep in the midst of wolves.
> Therefore be wise as serpents and harmless as doves. But beware
> of men, for they will deliver you up to councils and scourge you
> in their synagogues. You will be brought before governors and
> kings for My sake, as a testimony to them and to the Gentiles.
> But when they deliver you up, do not worry about how or what
> you should speak. For it will be given to you in that hour what
> you should speak; for it is not you who speak, but the Spirit of
> your Father who speaks in you."

When Jesus says, "Do not worry about how or what you should speak," does that sound like the disciples were depending on their great "knowledge" to reach unbelievers? Does it appear to you that the disciples had passed all of their exams through the Jesus Institute of Biblical Studies before being deployed into the harvest? I don't think so!

To the contrary, Jesus simply instructed the disciples that "it will be given to you in that hour what you should speak." After spending countless hours at the feet of Jesus, the disciples were still dependent on the Holy Spirit—just like us!

So what about the question of mobilization versus education? Which should come first? According to the example of Jesus, the correct answer is both! But how can that be?

It starts with a deeper understanding related to the process of discipleship. People cannot be properly trained as disciples unless they are placed into real-life situations that will force them to overcome their fears and desire to grow spiritually. In other words, I do not believe that Jesus "educated" the disciples then "mobilized" them into the field upon graduating with a seminary class in evangelism or worship.

As I read Jesus' actions and words (especially in Matt 10:16–20), it seems to me that He simultaneously "educated" the disciples as He sent them out into the fields. I believe the greatest times of discipleship with Jesus took place around the fire at night when they sought real life answers from Jesus in order to return to the harvest fields the next morning. By doing so, they were mentored out of the overflow of their experiences and were effectively trained to become worshippers who reproduced themselves into the lives of both believers and unbelievers.

This does not mean, however, that it is somehow wrong to seek knowledge and to further your "education" as part of becoming a mature disciple of Christ. Possessing a spiritual hunger and a desire to grow in understanding should be expected of all Christians. Nevertheless, if that knowledge is absorbed without the expectation of becoming a mature worshipper who yearns to join Christ on mission as a reproducing disciple, what is the point? In the end, a discipleship process that depends on education alone without simultaneous and consistent mobilization into the harvest fields will result in apathetic worshippers who are indifferent to the urgency of the Great Commission.

The Fallacy of Linear vs. Cyclical Discipleship

Much like the arguments presented above, the misleading concept of a *linear discipleship* grows from the idea that true worshippers are created through a discipleship process that emphasizes a lifetime of intense training—usually in a protected environment like the church building. Unfortunately, as evidenced by the anemic evangelistic practices of most Christians, the result is a generation of believers who pursue biblical knowledge without the expectation of joining Christ on mission as He seeks to "save the lost" (Luke 19:10 NRSV).

Trust me, after observing this practice for over thirty years of public ministry, it does not create biblical worshippers with a desire to make disciples. As noted in diagram 1 on page 138, regrettably, the linear approach has become the accepted process of discipleship in many Christian circles.

This process begins at the point of salvation when the church's first requirement for the new believer is to complete a multiweek discipleship book that rarely if ever mentions evangelism. In most cases there are long Bible studies explaining theological and even institutional requirements for becoming "good" Christians! While admittedly it is an overstatement to imply that the Great Commission is never mentioned, the subject is usually not a major emphasis. Evangelism is often presented as a watered down suggestion rather than a command.

The implication is that new Christians are not capable of being effective multipliers without first achieving an extremely high level of competency. Unfortunately, this linear process is a reoccurring theme in the lives of Christians as they are absorbed into the institutional church. Consider for a moment how many times you have been herded into discipleship classes related to handling personal finances, learning to pray, raising godly children, knowing God's will, and understanding your spiritual gifts. While these subjects are important to your personal growth, informational classes can create a false perception that spiritual maturity is achieved in the mind without feeling an urgency to join Christ on mission by taking the gospel back to our neighborhoods, workplaces, schools, and so forth.

The sad result of linear discipleship is a generation of church members who claim the name of Christ while ignoring the Great Commission. After all, if discipleship exists on a linear plain that ultimately ends in heaven and training classes are perceived as required steps to one's eternal reward, it is easy to understand why so

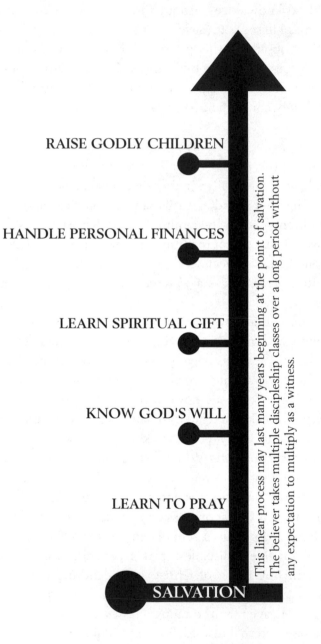

Diagram 1. Linear Discipleship

many Christians feel justified in their narcissistic faith that excludes the command to reproduce oneself through evangelism.

On the other side of this debate is the biblical concept of cyclical discipleship. You may recall that back in the first chapter, we discussed 12 misconceptions about evangelism. Number 5 stated that evangelism is not "in competition with discipleship." It was explained as follows:

> I often hear people espousing the tenets of discipleship over the call to evangelize. These people often minimize evangelism and use phrases like "I am a disciple maker, not an evangelist." This may sound good, but it is biblically incorrect. The truth is, evangelism and discipleship are uniquely dependent on each other. While intentional evangelism that leads to a spiritual conversion always precedes the process of discipleship, neither process is complete until the one who is being discipled learns to multiply their witness through sharing Christ with unsaved people. Possessing a genuine passion for biblical multiplication through evangelism is a key indicator when evaluating spiritual maturity.

The key phrase relating to the idea of discipleship being cyclical rather than linear is the statement, "Neither process [discipleship or evangelism] is complete until the one who is being discipled learns to multiply their witness through sharing Christ with unsaved people." In short, it is impossible to achieve biblical discipleship as a true worshipper without being personally connected to the call of the Great Commission.

When a person responds to the gospel and is genuinely redeemed, he or she is immediately connected to the process of becoming a reproducing disciple. Since the ultimate goal of discipleship should always be to reproduce more disciples, evangelism and discipleship are dependent on each other. Therefore, evangelism is much more than seeking "decisions" and sharing gospel presentations. Discipleship is much more than simply "training" people to memorize Bible verses. As noted in diagram 2 on page 141, neither the process of evangelism nor discipleship is complete unless they intentionally "cycle" together with the goal of leading the person who is evangelized into becoming a reproducing worshipper.

Without this full cycle of reproduction being evident in a person's life, I believe he or she is hard pressed to wear the name of Christ with dignity. If the goal is to become a worshipper of God, then obedience must be the driving force. How can there be obedience to Christ without joining Him on mission as His witnesses (Acts 1:8)?

In Matt 10:16–20 Jesus admits that He sent the disciples "out as sheep in the midst of wolves." It occurs to me that Jesus viewed the concept of evangelism as a perfect process to achieve mature discipleship among His rag-tag followers. He knew the disciples were going to be challenged, attacked, wounded, and possibly killed. Yet, He still sent them out to proclaim the message of hope.

By doing so, the disciples were forced to address a myriad of theological issues ranging from legalism to paganism. It is fair to say that Jesus expected reproduction from His disciples. This is why I believe that Jesus' primary approach to discipleship was evangelism. As I tell my classes, it appears to me that He discipled "to" evangelism "through" evangelism. Because He had limited earthly time with His disciples, Jesus' main pursuit was to create a movement that would glorify His Father and spread the gospel across the globe.

Jesus would have rejected the linear approach in favor of the cyclical discipleship model. While He obviously valued teaching and learning, Jesus had a singular goal—the fulfillment of the Great Commission.

If you do not believe this to be true, I suggest that you consider carefully the final words of Christ as expressed in Acts 1:8 (NASB):

> "But you will receive power when the Holy Spirit has come
> upon you; and you shall be My witnesses both in Jerusalem, and
> in all Judea and Samaria, and even to the remotest part of the
> earth."

Keep in mind that before making this statement, Christ rejects the earthly desire of the disciples to know about His kingdom. He quickly brings the discussion back to His greatest passion—to send

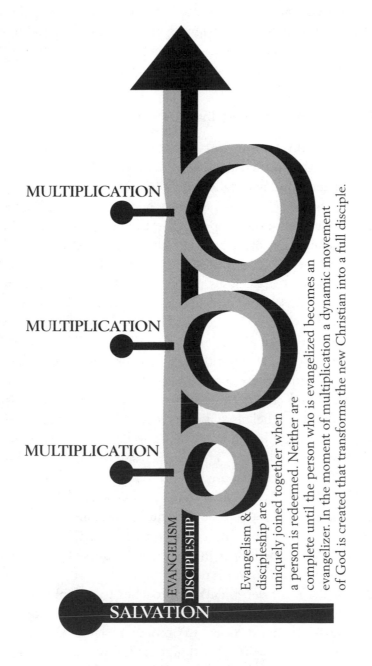

MULTIPLICATION

MULTIPLICATION

MULTIPLICATION

EVANGELISM

DISCIPLESHIP

SALVATION

Evangelism & discipleship are uniquely joined together when a person is redeemed. Neither are complete until the person who is evangelized becomes an evangelizer. In the moment of multiplication a dynamic movement of God is created that transforms the new Christian into a full disciple.

Diagram 2. Cyclical Discipleship

forth an obedient army of committed worshippers who would reproduce themselves through proclaiming salvation to a lost and hurting
world. When this naturally occurs among God's people, the cyclical
process of evangelism and discipleship are complete.

The Response of Service vs. the Call to Become Slaves

In Mark 10:42–45, Jesus instructs His disciples to become "servants"
in response to the entitled attitudes of James and John, who desire to
sit at Jesus' left hand and right hand when He enters into His glory.
He goes further with His instructions when He contrasts the idea of
being a "servant" with the deeper concept of being the "slave of all."

In this context, it must be noted that becoming a "servant" and
becoming a "slave" are both issues related to what it means to "be"
a true disciple of Christ. Jesus places an exclamation point on His
response to the disciples when He states in verse 45 (NKJV), "For
even the Son of man did not come to be served, but to serve, and to
give His life as a ransom for many."

It is hard to argue with Jesus' logic or His desire that true
disciples would ultimately become "slaves" who are fully surrendered
to the nature and call of Christ. Jesus knew that the world would
always challenge the beliefs and intentions of His followers. The best
response is to totally forfeit one's rights and become a "slave" to the
model of unconditional love and service espoused by Jesus through
His daily life as recorded in the New Testament.

This attitude of surrender and compassion has to become
incarnational in order to produce genuine disciples. Ultimately, it
goes back to the old debate of "being" versus "doing." In other words,
is a person a true worshipper just because he does the right acts of
service? The obvious answer is no!

One of the most detrimental approaches to discipleship occurs
when a new believer is simply instructed to serve without the
understanding of what it means to become a "slave." The end result
is a person who "does" the right things for the wrong reasons. If not
addressed, the person will not become a mature worshipper. The

person will wrongly seek to validate their faith by doing "stuff" for God without the intrinsic motivation to reproduce their lives by joining Christ on mission.

A disciple should serve, not because it is their duty, or that they are trying to get something from God as James and John attempted in Mark 10. A true worshipper serves because they have the heart of a "servant" and the surrendered will of a "slave."

At the End of the Day, Worship Is Reproducible

As mentioned back in chapter 3, Great Commission worship is reproducible. Our goal is to promote and bring into the body of Christ (the church) citizens from every tribe, tongue, culture, nation, and people group. Why? So that they might become worshippers, too! The principles of 2 Tim 2:1–3 and the role we have as worshipping evangelists are forever tied to the responsibility we have to disciple:

> My son, be strong in the grace that is in Christ Jesus. And the things that you have heard from me among many witnesses, commit these to faithful men who will be able to teach others also. You therefore must endure hardship as a good soldier of Jesus Christ. (NKJV)

The mandate is to go into all of the world and make fully devoted followers of Christ—true worshippers of God. This is putting feet on the missional aspect of Great Commission worship. Discipleship is critical to the success of Great Commission worship. This means we become part of the transformation process as we teach, train, develop, and nurture new worshippers. Contextualization becomes reality. We relate our message to culture. We live out in our lives principles of lifestyle evangelism and worship. We communicate the Word of God by the way we live. Therefore, Great Commission worship is reproducible.

The key to becoming a reproducible worshipper is to understand fully the influence you possess as a disciple of Christ. Through the power of the Holy Spirit, you can make an eternal difference in the lives of other people.

With this in mind, I was deeply impacted by an illustration I read in the book *Evangelism Is*. Under the heading, "Never Underestimate the Power of One," the following analogy is presented:

> One Samaritan woman testified to her town, and many believed in Jesus. One man, Noah, built a boat that saved the human race. One man, Moses, stood up to Pharaoh and delivered the Hebrews from Egypt. One woman, Deborah, delivered Israel from the Canaanite oppression. One man, David, defeated the Philistines when he killed their champion, Goliath. One woman, Esther, had the courage to approach the king and see her nation spared from extermination. One man, Peter, preached a sermon that led 3,000 to be saved. One salesman and Sunday school teacher, Edward Kimball, led a young man named Dwight to Christ. Dwight Moody became a blazing evangelist who, it is said, led one million souls to Christ in his short lifetime. Wilbur Chapman received the assurance of his salvation after talking with Moody and went on to become a noted evangelist himself. The drunken baseball player Billy Sunday was an assistant to Chapman before becoming the most famous evangelist of his day. One of the fruits of Sunday's ministry was the forming of a group of Christian businessmen in Charlotte, North Carolina. This group brought the evangelist Mordecai Ham to Charlotte in 1934. A tall, awkward youth named Billy Graham was converted during those meetings. According to his staff, as of 1993, more than 2.5 million people had "stepped forward at his crusades to accept Jesus Christ as their personal Savior." Millions of souls trace their spiritual lineage back to the influence of one man, a simple Sunday school teacher, Edward Kimball. Someone said, "To the world you may just be one person, but to one person you may be the world." To this we might add, to you they may seem

like just one lost soul, but to God that may be a soul who can shake the whole world.[3]

A true worshipper is created only when the "Power of One" becomes the "Power of One Multiplied." With the Great Commission as the backdrop, this intentional process of reproduction is essential in order to complete the cycle of biblical discipleship. The author further illustrates this point in a follow-up paragraph titled, "Never Underestimate the Power of One Multiplied." He quotes Walter Henrichsen:

> Some time ago there was a display at the Museum of Science and Industry in Chicago. It featured a checkerboard with 1 grain of wheat on the first, 2 on the second, 4 on the third, then 8, 16, 32, 64, 128, etc. Somewhere down the board, there were so many grains of wheat on the square that some were spilling over into neighboring squares—so here the demonstration stopped. Above the checkerboard display was a question, "At this rate of doubling every square, how much grain would be on the checkerboards by the 64th square?" To find the answer to this riddle, you punched a button on the console in front of you, and the answer flashed on a little screen above the board: "Enough to cover the entire subcontinent of India 50 feet deep." Multiplication may be costly, and in the initial stages, much slower than addition, but in the long run, it is the most effective way of accomplishing Christ's Great Commission and the only way.[4]

Great Commission worship is reproducible. We must remember, "when we lead people to Christ, we must stay with them to help them get established in their faith; then they can also be carriers of

---

[3] Earley and Wheeler, *Evangelism Is*, 133–34. Information in the quote came from, W. R. Moody, *The Life of Dwight L. Moody, by His Son* (New York: Fleming H. Revell, 1900), taken from the back cover; http://www.wheaton.edu/bgc/archives/faq/13htm; and "God's Billy Pulpit," *Time*, November 15, 1993, http://205.188.238.109/time/magazine/article/0,9171,979573,00.html.

[4] Ibid., 134. Quote taken from W. Henrichsen, *Disciples Are Made Not Born* (Carol Stream, IL: Victor Books, 1979), 143.

the good news and the message of the gospel will multiply through their consistent witness."[5] When this process of multiplication finally occurs, it is safe to assume that a Great Commission Worshipper is born!

Discussion Questions

1. How is Jesus' incarnation important in reference to the way Christians should live their daily lives?

2. What is the difference between mobilization and education, and how does each impact the way churches disciple new Christians?

3. What is the difference between linear and cyclical discipleship? Which approach is biblical?

4. What is the danger of the "service" mentality as opposed to becoming a "slave"? What is the difference, and why is this important?

5. Explain what it means to say that Great Commission worship is reproducible?

---

[5] Ibid.

CHAPTER 10

Great Commission Worship Is Reproducible . . .

Developing a Great Commission Worshipper (Part 2)

> *The disciple of Jesus is not the deluxe or heavy-duty model of the Christian—especially padded, textured, streamlined, and empowered for the fast lane on the straight and narrow way. (Rather) he stands on the pages of the New Testament as the first level of basic transportation in the kingdom of God.*
>
> Dallas Willard[1]

In order to become a Great Commission Worshipper, a Christian must understand the essential principles that are involved in becoming a reproducing disciple. Spiritual maturity that multiplies does not

---

[1] Dallas Willard, "Discipleship: For Super Christians Only," *Christianity Today* (October 10, 1980): 24.

occur by accident. It is an intentional progression of self-discovery in relation to the desires of Christ for His church.

The Process of Creating
a Reproducing Great Commission Worshipper

From Indifference to Incarnation

There is no doubt that the spirit of indifference is killing the church. I call it the reversal of the "Little House on the Prairie Syndrome." In case you were born after 1985, *Little House on the Prairie* was a hit show in the 1970s and early 1980s. Along with being shown in syndication for almost 30 years, there have also been numerous follow-up specials that have kept the fictional small town of "Walnut Grove" on the minds of fans across the world. The star of the show was Michael Landon.

The show was a depiction of life in rural America in the 1800s. It was popular in that era to have community buildings that served multiple purposes. I found it interesting that in Walnut Grove the school (grades 1–8) and the local church met in the same place as did almost all other community functions. Because the church was seen as part of the fabric of Walnut Grove, it naturally played an influential role in helping to set the spiritual climate for the local community.

You could say that the "Church at Walnut Grove," as it might be known today, was an incarnational expression of Christ in their community! To borrow a phrase used in the previous chapter, they "pitched their tent" in the midst of meeting community needs. In times of celebration or famine, the church was everything but indifferent to the people of Walnut Grove.

Unfortunately, this is no longer the case. I believe indifference has become the norm for many congregations today. Rather than embracing people's needs, we choose to remain removed from the front lines of ministry. This has negatively impacted the way the church does its discipleship. It reminds me of a slogan I saw on a T-shirt a few years ago: "If you need anything, don't hesitate to ask someone else."

The church seems to be making similar statements every time they criticize the world for acting sinful. It seems that indifference is not only accepted in the church, it is promoted as normal behavior. Note how my good friend, John Avant, explains this attitude of indifference:

> I preached at a conference recently. I gave the people a simple way to judge whether their church was really committed to missions. I said, "If you have a missionary come and tell you a story of reaching hundreds of children with AIDS in Africa, you'll cry and applaud, but what will happen to your church if your pastor brings in hundreds of African Americans or hundreds of people with AIDS?" Awkward silence filled the room. The whole world has changed around us. Every church sits in the middle of a mission field. The diversity of races, cultures, religions, philosophies, and worldviews has grown so rapidly that it is shocking. You live on the mission field, but the truth is that most of Christianity is not terribly interested in Jesus' mission. Fulfilling that mission would require so much change from the current club regulations that one thing becomes clear to the doorkeepers: if they let this change in, the club will never be the same. It will not even resemble what it has been, and that is just too much to bear. So we appoint a professional class of missionaries to do the dirty work for us, and we make sure that the dirty work they do stays far enough from the front doors of our church buildings to avoid the nasty reminders that we ourselves are supposed to be doing something on this mission. We either celebrate the missionaries as distant heroes or forget that they are even out there at all. Either way, we're free of the burden.[2]

For the sake of developing reproducing incarnational disciples, this attitude of selfish indifference must be eradicated from the realm of acceptable behavior for all Christians.

---

[2] John Avant, *If God Were Real* (New York: Howard Books, 2009), 64.

In a sense, the concepts of indifference and incarnation create polar extremes on the scale of discipleship. There are the stereotypical church members who moves through life with little regard for the needs of hurting people. Their concept of worship and evangelism is limited to the church building on Sunday morning. They are somehow conditioned to be indifferent for lack of biblical discipleship that challenges them to become reproducers of their faith. These people believe that real ministry should be reserved for paid staff members— not farmed out to busy church goers. They are loyal to the institution of the church as long as it does not interfere with their daily lives. On the other end of the spectrum is the idea of developing reproducing incarnational disciples. As Avant states:

> If we really believed God, everyone would be on the mission.
> In fact, I believe that the mission would be the very core of the
> church's DNA. No follower of Christ would be able to make any
> sense out of life lived apart from the mission of loving, serving,
> and sharing the good news with those who are not yet followers
> of Christ.[3]

Incarnational disciples do not require being prodded by a pastor or church leader to be involved in ministry. They have a keen understanding that the church is not a building or a location, but the people of God. Incarnational worshippers understand their faith to be an expression of what it means to be a follower of Christ. Evangelism and worship, therefore, are a "calling" to be lived out and reproduced through their daily routines. Ultimately, real worshippers are motivated by obedience rather than duty.

Progressive Levels of What It Means to Be a True Worshipper[4]

Oscar Thompson was a pastor for 20 years before joining the faculty at Southwestern Baptist Theological Seminary in Fort Worth, Texas,

---

[3] Ibid., 68.
[4] Parts of this section, including the introduction, "It Is Who You Know," and "Concentric Circles and Creating Disciples," are taken from *Evangelism Is*, 196–202.

as professor of evangelism. Before dying of cancer in 1980, Oscar left a treasure of wisdom for those of us charged with sharing the gospel and making biblical disciples (worshippers).

His wisdom was published in a popular book called *Concentric Circles of Concern*.

I cannot overemphasize the massive influence this book has had on my life and ministry. I recall reading it for the first time in seminary. My wife can affirm that I drove her crazy that afternoon by interrupting her television and naptime every few minutes with a new insight. Thompson's approach of viewing evangelism and discipleship as singular entities was transformational in light of the 1980s church growth movement that often valued numbers and addition over embracing a mentality of reproduction and disciple-making.

His notion of relationship evangelism is a helpful way of understanding and explaining how God reaches people with the gospel through relationships. Thompson believed "He [God] wants to love your world through you and to draw it to Him."[5] The diagram below shows the radius of relationships in our lives. Each circle from the center represents a slightly more distant relationship.

Diagram 1. Concentric Circles

---

[5] W. O. Thompson Jr., *Concentric Circles of Concern: Seven Stages for Making Disciples* (Nashville: B&H, 1999), 9.

It Is Who You Know

Each Christian occupies circle 1: "self." We are surrounded by people we can influence with the message of Christ. These people fall into one of six concentric circles around us. The closest circle to us is our "Immediate Family" in circle 2, followed by our "Relatives" in circle 3, and our "Friends" in circle 4. "If our relationship with the Lord is genuine," Thompson says, "we will want to share the good news of Christ with those closest to us." Circle 5 includes "Neighbors and Associates," followed by "Acquaintances" in circle 6. The outermost ring (circle 7) represents strangers, which the author refers to as "Person X." While the intended focus of Thompson's approach was to encourage Christians to seek out "Person X" intentionally, Thompson observed another more powerful phenomenon. Those in his classes were reaching people in their first four circles—family, relatives, friends, and neighbors. He observed that this "happened only as God's people were led to share the gospel with the people they were closest to."[6] He found that we reach people through relationships.

Concentric Circles and Creating Disciples (Worshippers)

Thompson's second major emphasis aimed at explaining how to make genuine disciples of those individuals in the circles of influence. The process has seven stages:

Stage 1. Get Right with God, Self, and Others

Thompson said, "A person can never lead another closer to the Lord than he or she already is. Evangelism must flow from a life that is deeply in love with the Lord."[7]

---

[6] Ibid., 2.
[7] W. O. Thompson Jr., C. King, and C. T. Ritzmann, *Witness to the World* (Nashville, TN: LifeWay, 2008), 9.

Thompson believed that the most important word in the English language is *relationship*. If love is the train, he says, "relationship is the track."[8] For Thompson, evangelism is supremely relational.

The most important relationship is our relationship with God. We must come to God on His terms, make Him Lord of our lives, and receive His gift of salvation. Once we are right with God, we need to examine our relationships with others and restore them if necessary. No one can be right with God and still be wounded by broken relationships.

Stage 2. Survey Your Relationships

In this stage Christians are encouraged to examine their circles of relationships in order to identify individuals in need of Christ's love and salvation. We may not realize how many people God has put within our reach. Once we start to identify these individuals, we should gather basic information that will guide both our prayers and efforts to reach out to them.

Stage 3. Work with God Through Prayer

Prayer is not just a warm-up exercise before you do your spiritual work, but intimate fellowship with a holy God who desires close and frequent prayer time with His children. Through these intimate times you will gain the wisdom and discernment to recognize opportunities for making disciples.

Stage 4. Build Relationship Bridges to People

As you pray for those people in your concentric circles, you will learn to recognize unsaved individuals. In response you should intentionally begin to build bridges to those people that God has put in your

---

[8] Ibid., 2.

path. This enables God's love to flow through you with the goal of leading them to Christ.

Stage 5. Show God's Love by Meeting Needs

When you show God's love to a needy world, it becomes a visual evidence that He is working in your heart to love people you otherwise might not seek to know. Meanwhile, God is working in those you are praying for and connecting with so that you will become a conduit of God's unending love as He draws hurting people to Himself.

Stage 6. Make Disciples and Help Them Grow

In this stage Thompson outlines the role of the Holy Spirit. We are to be witnesses for Christ and to share our faith, but the Holy Spirit's role is to convict them of sin and show them the truth of the gospel. If they choose to yield to Christ, we (and other Christians) need to help them develop a personal relationship with Jesus Christ through consistent prayer and reading His Word.

Stage 7. Help New Christians Make Disciples

The final stage is the beginning of the cycle for new Christians. Once they have become Christ-followers, encourage them to survey the people in their concentric circles. They should immediately begin praying for them, mending broken relationships, building relational bridges, and showing God's love in practical ways. The ultimate goal is to multiply through leading others to become authentic disciples.[9]

---

[9] Thompson, *Concentric Circles of Concern*, 35. In reference to stages 1–7, see pages 30–34.

The Five Levels of Progression to Becoming a Reproducing Worshipper

It is helpful to see the levels of Thompson's process for creating disciples (worshippers). This gives us a greater foundation from which to evaluate contemporary evangelism and discipleship. His desire, like mine, is to create incarnational disciples who ultimately desire to reproduce their lives and to expand God's kingdom.

In order to do this, we will use five levels to explain the progression of becoming a biblical worshipper. In honor of Thompson we will use five of his seven relational circles in reverse order to explain how Christians should be motivated to move away from a mind-set that serves the institutional church. It is "hard for institutional Christianity to do anything but protect itself."[10] Therefore, the goal is to become passionate believers who see the church through the eyes of reproduction and compassion, rather than the protector of dry orthodoxy and unbiblical traditions.

With this in mind, the following levels should be viewed as descending steps to spiritual maturity. Assuming the person professes to be a Christian, the process begins with the most shallow and least committed church-goers and moves to a worshipper who is fully engaged with all tenants of his faith. The goal is to create Great Commission Worshippers who are fully committed to Christ and His mission to reproduce Himself through His followers.

Keep in mind that the first three levels represent an "institutional" mind-set where Christians are encouraged to be involved in church "outreach" activities along with various other ministries to the exclusion of feeling any responsibility for impacting their workplaces, schools, homes, or neighborhoods. Levels 1–3 are driven by a deep sense of "duty" to God and the church rather than becoming "incarnational" disciples. The desire of a true worshipper is to multiply naturally from a heart of love and obedience. Note that levels 4 and 5 should be the ultimate destination for all Christians.

---

[10] Avant, *If God Were Real*, 66.

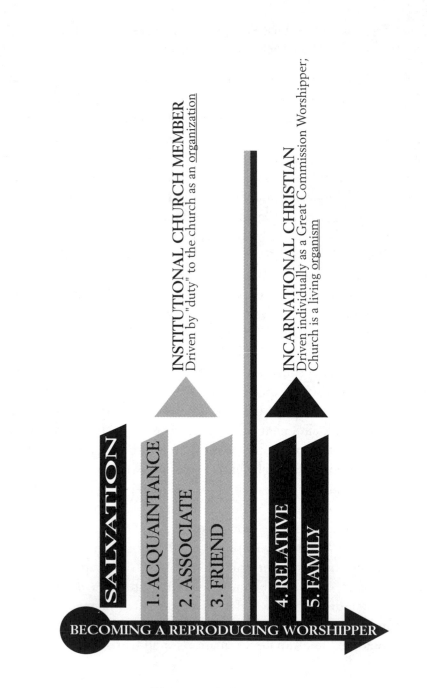

Diagram 2. Five Levels

For more information related to this process, you will want to see diagram 2 on page 156 and pay special attention to the explanation of the levels on the pages following.

Level 1. Acquaintance of Christ (Institutional)

An acquaintance can be defined as having "personal knowledge or information about someone or something" or "a relationship less intimate than friendship."[11] In reference to daily life situations, one person explained the idea of being an acquaintance by admitting, "I have trouble remembering the names of all my acquaintances."[12]

We all know what this person means. At some point, everyone meets an "acquaintance" and realizes they never asked the person's name. You recognize the face and perhaps the voice, but the level of personal intimacy is not what it could be.

Sadly, the same can be true with our Christian walk. A person at level 1 is at best a nominal believer. While they claim to have a relationship with Christ, it is usually defined by occasionally attending services on Sunday morning and participating in church-sponsored events a few times a year as long as those don't require speaking to someone else about their faith.

Level 2. Associate of Christ (Institutional)

An associate can be defined as "a person who joins with others in some activity or endeavor" or a person "who is frequently in the company of another."[13]

Obviously, an associate is closer in relationship than an acquaintance. While an acquaintance may attend church occasionally, an associate feels the "duty" never to miss services on Sunday morning. For the associate, church attendance is the apex of being a "good" Christian.

---

[11] See http://wordnetweb.princeton.edu/perl/webwn.
[12] Ibid.
[13] See http://wordnetweb.princeton.edu/perl/webwn.

Most of the time they see Christ as someone to "hang out with" as long as they remain in control. These people are what my sister calls "Christian store believers." You know the type. They have a fish on their car and Christian figurines in their office. They might even wear Christian t-shirts and crosses. In the end, "associate" believers are usually comfortable in their faith and often do not want to be challenged.

Level 3. Friend of Christ (Institutional)

This is a popular concept among many Christians. Jesus instructed His disciples in John 15:12–15 about the true dimensions of authentic friendship and love.

> "This is My commandment, that you love one another, just as I have loved you. Greater love has no one than this, that one lay down his life for his *friends*. You are My *friends* if you do what I command you. No longer do I call you slaves, for the slave does not know what his master is doing; but I have called you *friends*, for all things that I have heard from My Father I have made known to you." (NASB, italics added)

I must admit that it is comforting to think of Christ in terms of being my friend, but Jesus said, "You are My friends if you do what I command you."

In contemporary culture, I fear that the concept of friendship is not interpreted by Christians through the eyes of obedience to His commands. With the advent of social networks such as Facebook, the idea of being someone's friend is no longer an act of personal submission or intimacy. Being a person's friend is often a casual term that can be accepted or denied based on a person's preference. In the virtual world, it is normal to be someone's friend without the need for commitment or loyalty.

I am certain this is not the interpretation that Jesus desired when He told the disciples, "No longer do I call you slaves, for the slave does not know what his master is doing; but I have called you *friends*, for all things that I have heard from My Father I have made known to you."

Christians who make it to this level can be spiritually schizophrenic. These people usually appear to be well grounded in their faith. They are often church leaders such as deacons, teachers, or even pastors. Unfortunately, even though God is calling them away from the "institutional" model of faith that limits their influence to a geographical location ("the church building"), they hold on and refuse to move ahead with God for fear of removing the man-made chains of tradition and approval.

It is like standing on the highest mountain overlooking the promised land and feeling the call to freedom and real faith, but refusing to move. The danger arises if you linger too long. Before you know it, the taste of manna, while ordinary and bland, has become a comfort food attached to past memories.

In the end, level 3 Christians enjoy their friendship with Christ as long as the price of being His disciple doesn't go too high! They are willing to obey to a point. Many level 3 Christians know this attitude is detrimental to the cause of Christ, but they remain entrenched in the familiar, refusing to change. They can sense the call of Christ into a new covenant of freedom to "be" the reproducing church in flesh as a living organism. Yet sadly, they remain committed to the church as an institution to be protected and memorialized.

Level 4. Relative of Christ (Incarnational)

It is at this point that a worshipper transitions from the institutional model of living out the Christian life that focuses on the church as a location to the incarnational model that views the New Testament church as being a living organism. While this is a noteworthy transformation, the disciple is just beginning to understand spiritual reproduction.

For the first time, he or she is beginning to live the Great Commission, not just talk about it. The idea of being on mission with Christ takes on a whole new meaning. Faithfulness is no longer reserved for Sunday mornings. Evangelism is becoming a daily task through relationships rather than an assignment during a church-sponsored event.

The Christian life is no longer a duty to be checked off on a list of spiritual requirements. The Acts 1:8 call is taking on flesh, breath, and limbs, in order to be lived out and reproduced on a daily basis. What was once a drudgery to be endured is now becoming a privilege to join Christ on mission to impact the world.

Warning: A level 4 disciple presents a unique danger that must be addressed. Because this person is experiencing a new kind of spiritual freedom from the institutional church, it is possible for their zeal to send them in the wrong direction theologically and practically. Their potential for impacting the world for Christ is phenomenal, but it must be guided in the right direction. In some cases, the person might grow discouraged by the unwillingness of other Christian friends to share their excitement and repent from their addiction to the institutional church model. If the discouragement is not addressed, I have seen level 4 disciples walk away from the church, citing their defiance to organized religion and institutional hypocrisy. Close mentoring is essential at this level.

Level 5. Family Member of Christ (Incarnational)

Level 5 Christianity represents the desired expression of faith for all true worshippers. This is not to say, however, that the believer has reached the end of their spiritual growth. When a Christian arrives at the place in their spiritual walk where they see themselves as fully missional beings with an innate desire to incarnationally, sacrificially, and biblically express their faith regardless of the ramifications, this is what it means to wear the distinction of being family.

The key to becoming a level 5 worshipper is obedience and total surrender to the reproducing plan of Christ! This distinction of family is not easily obtained, nor is it easily maintained, even in the lives of seasoned believers.

This is evidenced by the testimonies of some well-known biblical characters. Their struggles are well documented in Scripture.

Consider the Story of Peter . . .

A good example of this spiritual transformation between levels 4 and 5 is the apostle Peter. For much of his early days spent with Christ, Peter was growing in his faith but remained misguided and self-absorbed. For example, consider what happens in Matt 16:16 after Jesus asks Peter in verse 15, "Who do you say that I am?" Like a pro, Peter responds on cue by saying, "You are the Christ, the Son of the living God." Jesus follows up in verse 17 by congratulating Peter: "Blessed are you, Simon Barjona, because flesh and blood did not reveal this to you, but My Father who is in heaven" (NASB).

At this point, things look pretty good for Peter. That is, until later in the same conversation, when Jesus foretells His eventual death and resurrection. Like many times before, Peter blindly responds to Jesus by taking Him aside and rebuking Him: "God forbid it, Lord! This shall never happen to You." It is then that Jesus turns to Peter and says, "Get behind Me, Satan! You are a stumbling block to Me; for you are not setting your mind on God's interests, but man's" (Matt 16:22–23 NASB).

Jesus then uses the naïve ramblings of Peter as a way to teach the disciples and us concerning the true cost of following Him. Note Matt 16:24–27 (NASB):

> Then Jesus said to His disciples, "If anyone wishes to come after Me, he must deny himself, and take up his cross and follow Me. For whoever wishes to save his life will lose it; but whoever loses his life for My sake will find it. For what will it profit a man if he gains the whole world and forfeits his soul? Or what will a man give in exchange for his soul? For the Son of Man is going to come in the glory of His Father with His angels, and WILL THEN REPAY EVERY MAN ACCORDING TO HIS DEEDS."

Peter makes a similar mistake in John 13. Just as before, Jesus is trying to prepare His disciples for His inevitable death and resurrection.

He goes on to express that He would only be with them a little while longer. Peter dialogues with Jesus in verses 36–38 (NASB):

> "Lord, where are You going?" Jesus answered, "Where I go, you cannot follow Me now; but you will follow later." Peter said to Him, "Lord, why can I not follow You right now? I will lay down my life for You." Jesus answered, "Will you lay down your life for Me? Truly, truly, I say to you, a rooster will not crow until you deny Me three times."

Of course, we all know what happened next. As Jesus predicted, a boisterous Peter denied Christ three times.

Only after Jesus' death and resurrection do we see the full transformation of Peter. The setting was a beach on the Sea of Tiberias. After a long night of fishing when Peter and the disciples caught nothing, they were approaching the seashore early in the morning. After receiving a quick lesson on fishing from an unknown man on the seashore, John peered through the fog and mist to finally proclaim that the mysterious man was actually the "Lord." Immediately Peter arose and dove into the water in order to approach Christ. According to John 21, not much was said until after breakfast when Jesus pulled Peter aside and asked the following three questions found in verses 15–17 (NASB):

> Jesus said to Simon Peter, "Simon, son of John, do you love Me more than these?" He said to Him, "Yes, Lord; You know that I love You." He said to him, "Tend My lambs." He said to him again a second time, "Simon, son of John, do you love Me?" He said to Him, "Yes, Lord; You know that I love You." He said to him, "Shepherd My sheep." He said to him the third time, "Simon, son of John, do you love Me?" Peter was grieved because He said to him the third time, "Do you love Me?" And he said to Him, "**Lord, You know all things**; You know that I love You." Jesus said to him, "Tend My sheep."

This passage is the key to Peter's ultimate transformation as a *family* level Christian. The key is the phrase, "Lord, You know all things." Until this point, Peter revealed flashes of maturing, but he remained conflicted and self-absorbed. He had to become a broken man, fully surrendered to Christ and willing to give up everything, before he could become the amazing evangelist we read about in the book of Acts!

Consider the Story of Paul . . .

We all know the amazing story of the apostle Paul. He was well-educated and extremely self-absorbed. At one time, Paul was leader of the ruling class of religious men in the temple. Note Phil 3:4b–6 (NASB):

> If anyone else has a mind to put confidence in the flesh, I far
> more: circumcised the eighth day, of the nation of Israel, of
> the tribe of Benjamin, a Hebrew of Hebrews; as to the Law,
> a Pharisee; as to zeal, a persecutor of the church; as to the
> righteousness which is in the Law, found blameless.

Yet it was Paul who was eventually transformed on the road to Damascus through an encounter with the risen Christ. From that point onward, Paul was sold out to Christ with the same vigor that he used to persecute the church.

His complete transformation as a *family* level (incarnational) believer can be characterized in the careful way he ministered to the Thessalonians in 1 Thess 2:1–12 (NASB, italics added):

> For you yourselves know, brethren, that our coming to you
> was not in vain, but after we had already suffered and been
> mistreated in Philippi, as you know, we had the boldness in our
> God to speak to you the gospel of God amid much opposition.
> For our exhortation does not come from error or impurity or
> by way of deceit; *but just as we have been approved by God to
> be entrusted with the gospel, so we speak, not as pleasing men, but
> God who examines our hearts.* For we never came with flattering
> speech, as you know, nor with a pretext for greed—God is
> witness—nor did we seek glory from men, either from you or
> from others, even though as apostles of Christ we might have
> asserted our authority. *But we proved to be gentle among you, as*

*a nursing mother tenderly cares for her own children. Having so
fond an affection for you, we were well-pleased to impart to you* **not
only the gospel of God but also our own lives,** *because you had
become very dear to us.* For you recall, brethren, our labor and
hardship, how working night and day so as not to be a burden
to any of you, we proclaimed to you the gospel of God. [10]You
are witnesses, and so is God, how devoutly and uprightly and
blamelessly we behaved toward you believers; *just as you know
how we were exhorting and encouraging and imploring each one of
you as a father would his own children, so that you would walk in a
manner worthy of the God who calls you into His own kingdom and
glory.*

Paul obviously understood his role as a Christian was to become a
reproducing *incarnational* follower of Christ. He was a proclaimer of
truth, "not as pleasing men, but God who examines our hearts." But
as he says, it was not through "flattering speech" or a sense of blind
duty to an institution. He was not proclaiming a religious lifestyle or
adherence to a set of legalistic rules.

Rather, the key to Paul's ministry is found in the words:

But we proved to be gentle among you, as a nursing mother
tenderly cares for her own children. Having so fond an affection
for you, we were well-pleased to impart to you not only the
gospel of God but also our own lives, because you had become
very dear to us.

If there were Skype in heaven, Paul would passionately implore
all of us to pay special attention to the way he lived out his faith
among the Thessalonians. The Bible uses words like *gentle* and *affection.* He also references phrases like "a nursing mother tenderly cares
for her own children" and "you had become very dear to us." Does
that sound like Paul was disconnected from his ministry field? On the
contrary, he states, "We were well-pleased to impart to you not only
the gospel of God but also our own **lives.**"

Paul is representative of level 5 living at its best! A *family* level
worshipper is completely sold out for Christ. He realizes that genuine

Christianity is a 24/7 existence that demands full allegiance to Christ and His Great Commission!

Such persons are committed to biblical reproduction and worship in its highest form. They are not looking to hire staff members to fulfill their responsibilities. Church attendance and adherence to meaningless traditions are not the capstones of their spiritual existence! On the contrary, they understand their spiritual calling as true worshippers and if necessary, are willing to die in the pursuit of that calling in order to glorify God and to impact the world for Christ! This should be the end goal of all Great Commission Worshippers!

Putting It All Together

This chapter is the second of three consecutive chapters aimed at explaining the characteristics and processes needed to become a reproducing biblical worshipper. Genuine discipleship should always reproduce incarnational Christians with a passion to fulfill the Great Commission, rather than mere followers of institutional religion.

The sad truth is that after years of settling for linear approaches to discipleship, we may be the most educated and least effective Christians in history. Without reestablishing the cycle of multiplication that combines discipleship with evangelism and worship, the church will continue to decline even further into a destructive attitude of indifference. Christ expects all of His children to share His heart for reaching the world with the gospel. Genuine disciples are always active (reproducing) participants in the Great Commission.

So, what's the point? Every true worshipper should naturally desire to wrap their faith in the flesh of daily living out the call of the gospel in every sphere of their life. The end result should be a life consumed by worship that is fueled by obedience to Christ and His invitation to become reproducible "fishers of men" (Mark 1:17).

Discussion Questions

1. Explain the difference between indifference and incarnation.

2. Discuss the importance of the seven concentric circles of essential relationships.

3. Discuss the three institutional levels of progression related to becoming a reproducing worshipper.

4. Discuss the two incarnational levels of progression related to becoming a reproducing worshipper.

5. Fully discuss the implications of the statement, "Christ expects all of His children to share His heart for reaching the world with the gospel."

CHAPTER 11

Great Commission Worship Is Reproducible . . .

Discipling the Great Commission Worshipper (Part 3)

> *While there were no professional missionaries devoting their whole life to this specific work, every congregation was a missionary society, and every Christian believer a missionary, inflamed by the love of Christ to convert his fellow men. Every Christian told his neighbor, the laborer told his fellow laborer, the slave to his fellow slave, the servant to his master and mistress, the story of his conversion as a mariner tells the story of the rescue from shipwreck.*
>
> Philip Schaff (about the early days of the post-apostolic church)[1]

The Great Commission at the end of Matthew's Gospel is perhaps the most often cited Scripture on creating disciples (worshippers).

---

[1] Philip Schaff, *History of the Christian Church*, vol. 2: *Anti-Nicene Christianity* (Grand Rapids: Eerdmans, 1910), 20–21.

Here Jesus gives a clear charge to His disciples and assures them of His continued spiritual presence.

> And Jesus came and said to them, "All authority in heaven and on earth has been given to me. Go therefore and make disciples of all nations, baptizing them in the name of the Father and of the Son and of the Holy Spirit, and teaching them to obey everything that I have commanded you. And remember, I am with you always, to the end of the age." (Matt 28:18–20 NRSV)

John's Gospel has a condensed version of Jesus commissioning His disciples: "as the Father has sent me, I am sending you" (John 20:21 NIV). The same is true in the book of Acts where Luke records Jesus' final instructions to His disciples before ascending to heaven: "but you will receive power when the Holy Spirit has come upon you; and you shall be My witnesses both in Jerusalem, and in all Judea and Samaria, and even to the remotest part of the earth" (Acts 1:8 NASB).

In the New Testament, Jesus uses the phrase, "Follow me" at least 20 times. The first time was probably to Phillip (John 1:43). In Matt 4:19 and Mark 1:17 Jesus told Simon Peter and his brother Andrew, "Follow me and I will make you fishers of men."

There is only one instance in the New Testament where the term *follower* is used (Acts 24:14). There are 294 references to "disciples" or "disciple." This suggests that once a person submits and obeys the call to follow Jesus and His Great Commission, they are considered disciples.

Yet, it is not enough simply to imitate Christ in order to become His disciple. Those who "follow Him" are called to reproduce through a lifestyle that *incarnationally* emulates Christ. According to the apostle Paul, "Put to death, therefore, whatever belongs to your earthly nature: sexual immorality, impurity, lust, evil desires and greed, which is idolatry" (Col 3:5–6 NIV).

This can also include "putting to death" an unwillingness to boldly confess Christ for fear of man's retribution. Consider John 12:41–42 (NASB):

Nevertheless many even of the rulers believed in Him, but because of the Pharisees they were not *confessing* Him, for *fear* that they would be put out of the synagogue; for they loved the approval of men rather than the approval of God.

Other attributes of a true disciple should include *self-denial* (Matt 16:2; Mark 8:34); *renunciation* (Mark 10:21,28); *sacrifice* (Luke 9:59,61; 14:33); *steadfastness* (John 8:31; 12:26); *fruitfulness* (John 15:8); and *love* (John 13:35).[2]

Disclaimer: The traditional approach to creating biblical worshippers consists of assigning some type of discipleship manual to be completed within the first eight to twelve weeks after a person becomes a Christian. The bulk of the daily Bible studies is usually focused upon helping the new believers to grasp essential aspects of their new faith. The basic concept assumes that the more persons are exposed to theological training through biblical exercises, the quicker their spiritual foundation will be solidified and they can become functioning members of a local church.

Herein lies the problem. The key phrase to consider is "functioning" member. To me, it is a simple issue of *information* verses *incarnation*. Unfortunately, almost all contemporary discipleship processes are driven solely by the *informational* model. From the point of a person's salvation this approach strives to get believers enrolled in discipleship studies that address issues such as money, parenting, spiritual gifts, etc. The common fallacy is that spiritual maturity can be achieved by education alone without *incarnationally* sending Christians back into their communities and workplaces to become reproducing worshippers.

In the following discipleship process, the components of *information* and *incarnation* join forces to create missional worshippers who are engaged in the Great Commission from the beginning point of salvation. To some of you, this will appear to be backwards. We have been conditioned in Christian circles to assume that new believers

---

[2] Michael R. Mitchell, *On Following Jesus*, Discipleship Ministries text (Lynchburg, VA: Liberty Baptist Theological Seminary, 2004), 1.

do not "know" enough to be effective multipliers. As a result, if evan-gelism is mentioned in a discipleship model, it is usually emphasized towards the end of the study and rarely plays a major role.

This is a mistake. Missional worshippers are not created in the classroom alone. They must embrace the process of engaging ministry as a daily lifestyle of active worship. It has been my experience that if new believers are discipled apart from the requirement of sharing their faith with unsaved friends, they will lose their passion and even-tually assume that the Great Commission is reserved for professional clergy. At best, these new believers will settle in as level 3 Christians and will never achieve their full spiritual potential as reproducing *incarnational* worshippers.

Building the Foundation to Become a Great Commission Worshipper

The Process Begins with the Great Commandment

From the point that a person becomes a Christian, the following pro-cess teaches the worshipper to embrace the Great Commandment to "love God" and to "love others." (See diagram 1 on the next page.)

This eternal concept grows directly from the words of Jesus when He was asked by a religious leader to pinpoint the greatest commandment. His simple response was to instruct His disciples to approach life in a profound manner. He states:

> "'You shall love the LORD your God with all your heart, with all your soul, and with all your mind.' This is the first and great commandment. And the second is like it: 'You shall love your neighbor as yourself.' On these two commandments hang all the Law and the Prophets." (Matt 22:37–40 NKJV)

If the purpose of life is to exalt Christ as obedient worshippers, then it makes sense that "loving God" should be the primary *motivation* of all Christians. "Loving others" must become the primary *mission*.

Worship Is the Central Focus

As noted in diagram 1 below, the expression of worship is the central focus of this discipleship process. After establishing the two essential prongs of "loving God" and "loving others," the backbone of the six-week process is learning to live a reproducing lifestyle of worship that is grounded in obedience to the Great Commandment and the Great Commission.

Without worship as the core, what is the point? Everything in this process connects back to the lifeline of exalting God above all else. Much as the frame of a car provides needed stability and protection, so worship provides a similar foundation from which a new believer can become a reproducing disciple. Worship is a constant track from which true disciples must never stray.

The Process to Become a Great Commission Worshipper

Contrary to traditional approaches to discipleship that assume new believers cannot be effective multipliers for a lack of knowledge, this approach is initiated from the point in which a person is converted. If the goal is to develop *incarnational* disciples, that cannot be achieved by limiting the exposure of new believers to evangelistic ministry

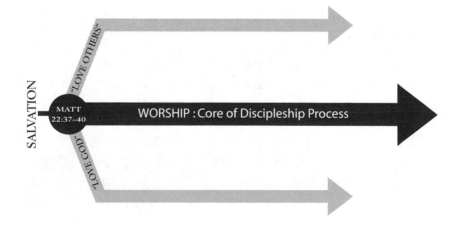

Diagram 1

opportunities. As mentioned earlier, I firmly believe that Jesus trained disciples through evangelism. Separating evangelism from discipleship will eventually weaken both.

The process is normally limited to the first six weeks after a person is converted. Since this is a critical time in a person's spiritual development, the intention is to establish a Great Commission lifestyle at a point when the new believer is most impressionable. The process is not intended to give the new Christian a crash course on every philosophy related to Christianity. It is, however, designed to avoid the trap of *linear* discipleship in favor of completing the *cycle* of spiritual reproduction. When and if this reproduction occurs, this process makes it much more likely that the new believer will eventually become a level 4 or level 5 Christian who *incarnationally* embraces their faith.

The process is designed to be taught on a regular basis through qualified mentors who have already graduated from the process. The key is regular accountability that encourages adherence to the daily and weekly assignments. We suggest that the maximum ratio should not be more than five students to one mentor. While this approach is primarily aimed at engaging new believers, **it can also be an effective means of refocusing seasoned Christians to reconnect with the Great Commission**.

Explaining the Six-Week Process

This process (see diagram on the next page) represents a culmination of what has been discussed in all of the previous chapters. You will note that all five steps to becoming a Great Commission Worshipper are integrated into the following discipleship template. They include; Formational (week 1), Transformational (week 2), Relational (week 3), Missional (week 4), and Reproducible (weeks 5 and 6). For the sake of being user friendly, each week will have *Incarnational* expressions; *Informational* Bible Studies; and *Ministry Equipping* assignments.

SALVATION

MATTHEW 22:37–40

"LOVE GOD"

"LOVE OTHERS"

WORSHIP : Core of Discipleship Process

	WEEK 1	WEEK 2	WEEK 3	WEEK 4	WEEK 5	WEEK 6
	FORMATIONAL	TRANSFORMATIONAL	RELATIONAL	MISSIONAL	REPRODUCIBLE	
	Tell someone every day what Christ has done for you	Tell someone every day what Christ has done for you	Tell someone every day what Christ has done for you	Tell someone every day what Christ has done for YOU	Tell someone every day what Christ has done for you	Tell someone every day what Christ has done for you
	7 BIBLE STUDIES on formational doctrine	7 BIBLE STUDIES on transformational concept of recovery	7 BIBLE STUDIES on relationship with God through prayer	7 BIBLE STUDIES on becoming a missional servant	7 BIBLE STUDIES on becoming a reproducible witness of the gospel	7 BIBLE STUDIES on imperatives of the faith: evangelism, involvement in a spiritual community, quiet time & living out personal righteousness
	ASSIGNMENT Prepare salvation testimony	ASSIGNMENT Prepare recovery testimony	ASSIGNMENT Create prayer list of unsaved people to pray for each day	ASSIGNMENT Begin to intentionally serve people on your prayer list	ASSIGNMENT Share gospel with at least 1 person you are serving & praying for daily	ASSIGNMENT Share gospel with 2 people you have been serving & praying for daily

Diagram 2

Week 1. Formational

Incarnational Expression. This is one of the essential components related to this model of discipleship. From day one the new convert is instructed to tell someone each day "what Christ has done for them." In the beginning, a simple testimony may be all that is needed. Something like "God is so good to me," or simply "God bless you" are acceptable the first week as the person is developing their salvation testimony. Obviously, the testimonies will become more involved as the person matures through the process.

Informational Bible Studies. This is where the *formational* process begins. During the first week, consider having seven simple Bible studies aimed at helping the new believer to understand the *formational* doctrines of the faith related to God the Father, Jesus Christ, the Holy Spirit, and so forth. The formational studies could come out of several key chapters in John's Gospel.

Ministry Equipping Assignment. The assignment for the first week is to help the believer to develop a salvation testimony. The goal is to prepare a one- to two-page outline of the person's salvation story. The basic outline should include three major points: (1) the person's life before meeting Christ as Savior; (2) how the person came to a saving relationship with Christ; (3) how the person's life has changed since surrendering their life to Christ. Obviously, if the person is a new believer, the third point may be limited.

If done well, the testimony will become an effective tool for connecting with unsaved friends, family, coworkers, and such. The testimony will evolve as the person begins to mature in faith. The hope is to arm new believers with a reproducible story of their spiritual journey to share as they daily connect with people in their spheres of influence.

Week 2. Transformational

Incarnational Expression: The new believer is instructed to continue telling a different person each day "what Christ has done for them."

Informational Bible Studies. This is where the *transformational* process takes over. During the second week, consider having seven simple Bible studies aimed at helping the new believer to understand the *transformational* experience of biblical recovery. The brief studies could come from biblical characters like David, Jonah, Paul, and Peter.

The key to the concept of recovery is to help the new believer to overcome their previous indiscretions. As a pastor and professor, I have found that one of the most lethal ways that Satan renders Christians unproductive spiritually is to constantly remind them of their past sins. What eventually happens is that every time the person starts to speak to someone about their faith, Satan reminds them of their unworthiness. This guilt serves to silence the Christian, thus limiting their impact with unsaved friends, family members, and coworkers.

For me, when it comes to recovery, I have always found it helpful to remember the words of the apostle Paul in Phil 3:13–14 (NASB):

> Brethren, I do not regard myself as having laid hold of it yet; but one thing I do: forgetting what lies behind and reaching forward to what lies ahead, I press on toward the goal for the prize of the upward call of God in Christ Jesus.

Ministry Equipping Assignment. The assignment for the second week is to help the believer to develop their recovery testimony. The one- to two-page summary should include three major points: (1) My life seemed normal until . . . ; (2) I discovered hope and help in Jesus when . . . ; (3) I am glad I have a personal relationship with Jesus today because . . .

The "Recovery Testimony" should explain a time when Jesus helped the person with a particular problem or need in his life. This is particularly helpful in bridging the gap to share the gospel with the unsaved. As a relational tool, this is even more effective than the salvation testimony. If you were suffering from an addiction or some type of malady, wouldn't you be more willing to listen to someone if they could relate to you situation? Over the years, I have had students who previously struggled with pornography or had chemical addictions. Some of the students were sexually abused as children, while others admitted their past anger with God over the death of a family member or the divorce of their parents. Others had experienced debilitating medical conditions like cancer or Lupus. In almost every instance, the students began to see their amazing stories of pain and bitterness through the new eyes of deliverance and freedom. As a result, they are now able to turn what Satan meant for harm into fresh tools to become reproducing worshippers.

Based on these experiences, I am convinced that the same *transformation* will happen in the lives of these new believers. And just like my students, through reading biblical stories about recovery, then preparing their testimonies, God will move them closer to becoming Great Commission Worshippers.

Week 3. Relational

Incarnational Expression. The new believer is instructed to continue telling a different person each day "what Christ has done for them." By this point, the new believer should be able to move beyond a simple "God bless you" or "God loves you" to a place where he or she is able to share more detailed encounters of "what God has done for them."

Informational Bible Studies. This is where the *relational* aspect of discipleship is formulated. There is no greater expression of relationship in a new Christian's life than the great need to abide in Christ through prayer. This is essential if we truly expect new believers to become Great Commission Worshippers.

Gregory Frizzell explains how this takes place:

> Friend, prayer is not primarily what we can get out of God, but what He purposes to do in and through us for His own pleasure. Prayer is a major way we come to know Him and hear His voice. Through prayer, we abide in Him and allow Him to live through us. Prayer is how Christ purifies His bride and builds His kingdom. The great secret of prayer is to align ourselves to God's purposes rather than seeking to align Him to ours. Until you are totally convinced of the importance of a lifestyle of prayer, you are not likely to take the necessary steps to achieve one. Above everything else, God desires a close personal relationship with each of His children. Yet, it is *impossible* to develop this

relationship without spending significant time with God. Prayer is the primary way you spend meaningful time with the Savior. Through prayer, God purposes to establish and deepen your personal relationship with Him.[3]

Escalating the spiritual life of the new believer requires a deep and abiding commitment to prayer. In order to get this relationship off the ground, I suggest seven Bible studies outlining various aspects of prayer. Aside from the Lord's Prayer (Matthew 6), you might also consider Jesus' prayer of submission in Gethsemane (Luke 22), Paul's prayer for the Ephesian believers (Ephesians 1 & 3), Abraham's prayer for Sodom (Genesis 18), Jesus' high priestly prayer (John 17), or David's prayer of confession (Psalm 51).

Ministry Equipping Assignment. The basic assignment for this week is to begin keeping a list of unsaved people and commit to pray for them daily. The list can include friends, family members, neighbors, and such.

Since the new believer is already sharing a brief testimony with a new person every day, how about beginning the list with several names from those daily encounters? The goal is twofold: (1) to fall in love with Christ and His missionary calling through prayer; and (2) to love the unsaved enough to regularly bring them before Christ through prayer. The end result will be an unmistakable burden to become a reproducing Great Commission Worshipper.

Week 4. Missional

Incarnational Expression. The new believer is instructed to continue telling a different person each day "what Christ has done for them." Week four represents a transition from merely speaking about Christ and His wonders to actually living out this faith by taking the next step to perform acts of service.

Informational Bible Studies. This is where the *missional* process begins. According to Ed Stetzer and Dave Putman in the book,

---

[3] Gregory R. Frizzell, *How to Develop a Powerful Prayer Life* (Memphis, TN: The Master Design, 1999), 2–3.

Breaking the Missional Code, "How we do mission flows from our understanding of God's mission."[4] At the same time, "having a missional heart is not enough."[5] We must possess a biblical foundation that directs our daily behavior as authentic servants.

In order to establish this strong biblical foundation as a motivation to become missional disciples, consider leading seven interactive Bible studies focusing on Mark 10 where Jesus corrects the entitled attitudes of James and John; John 13 where Jesus washes the disciples' feet; John 4 where Jesus speaks to the harlot woman at the well; and possibly two separate studies from Luke 10 where Jesus shares the parable of the Good Samaritan and expounds on the motivations of Mary and Martha. The key is to help new believers to understand their role as Great Commission Worshippers.

Ministry Equipping Assignment. Each week of this process grows in responsibilities related to becoming a missional Christian. In week four, the stakes are raised much higher with the expectation of actually beginning to serve the people whose names appear on the prayer list. This can be achieved in numerous ways. What if one of the people on the prayer list was a neighbor? How about surprising them by mowing their yard or cooking them a meal? One could also volunteer to babysit or simply begin by asking these neighbors if they had prayer needs.

The point of this exercise is to further develop an incarnational lifestyle that views serving as an involuntary compulsion to be adopted by missional believers. We should not serve because it is our duty. We should serve because we cannot help it! Not to do so would violate our spiritual conscience! Loving others through authentic service is an essential component in becoming a Great Commission Worshipper.

---

[4] Ed Stetzer and Dave Putman, *Breaking the Missional Code: Your Church Can Become a Missionary in Your Community* (Nashville: B&H, 2006), 15.

[5] Ibid.

Week 5. Reproducible

Incarnational Expression. As in past weeks, the believer is instructed to continue telling a different person each day "what Christ has done for them."

Becoming a *Reproducible* believer is the natural progression in learning to live the *missional* lifestyle as a Great Commission Worshipper. By this time, not only is the believer learning to engage people daily with brief testimonies and seeking out servant opportunities, but they now will begin learning the basics required to verbally communicate the gospel message.

Informational Bible Studies. In keeping with the progression above, this week should consist of seven Bible studies that briefly outline the essentials needed to verbally communicate the gospel message. The studies could include a brief overview of the Ten Commandments along with simple explanations of Romans 3, 5, 6, and 10. John 3 and Revelation 3 might also be helpful. At this point, the key is to build upon the person's enthusiasm and to make it user friendly and fun. "Thou shalt not overwhelm" has to be the guiding principle!

Ministry Equipping Assignment. In Philemon 6, the apostle Paul encourages us as growing disciples with the words, "I pray that the sharing of your faith may become effective for the full knowledge of every good thing that is in us for the sake of Christ" (ESV). This is similar to the final earthly words of Christ in Acts 1:8 when he instructs His disciples, "But you will receive power when the Holy Spirit has come upon you; and you will be my witnesses in Jerusalem, in all Judea and Samaria, and to the ends of the earth" (NRSV). By these and other biblical passages, it is obvious that verbally sharing our faith was greatly important to Christ just as it was to the early church. Therefore, if we are seeking to become obedient worshippers, we must do the same.

As mentioned above, the key is to build upon the persons' enthusiasm and to create biblical habits early in the disciple-making process. So what is the assignment? As the persons progress through the week and continue to serve and connect with people daily, *they*

*are instructed to utilize their testimonies as bridges to communicating the
gospel with at least one unsaved person.*

It has been my experience over 30 years of ministry that nothing
will profoundly impact a Christian's life more than joining hands with
the Holy Spirit and faithfully sharing Christ! This is especially true
when these same friends and family members surrender to Christ as
Lord. At that point, what is natural becomes supernatural, and what
is ordinary becomes extraordinary. The person will never be the same.

Week 6. Reproducible

Incarnational Expression. As in past weeks, the believer is instructed
to continue telling a different person each day "what Christ has done
for them."

Informational Bible Studies. We have finally arrived at the
concluding week of this initial discipleship process. From week 1
onward, the purpose has been to help the new believer to become
a Great Commission Worshipper. Each week, the Bible studies
have been crafted in order to intertwine with the learning activities
in order to create incarnational disciples who are engaged in their
ministry field from the initial point of salvation. The aim is a balance
between training the new believers intellectually and sending them
out incarnationally.

The purpose of week 6 is to continue the theme of the previous
week, to become *reproducible* in life and ministry. In week 5, this
meant equipping the new believers to share their faith using various
passages of Scripture.

Since this is the final week, it will be used to hammer home some
reproducible imperatives of the faith. This should include at least
one Bible study presenting evangelism as a command (possibly Acts
1:8 or Philemon 6). There also need to be two more Bible studies
explaining the imperative to be involved in the spiritual community
of a local congregation. The final four Bible studies should cover the
importance of developing a daily time in the Word and the imperative
to live out a life of righteousness.

Each of the Bible studies should include a challenge to multiply oneself through Christ by intentionally engaging in the lives of others. As the Great Commandment says:

> "You shall love the LORD your God with all your heart, with all your soul," and with all your mind . . . and the second is like it: 'You shall love your neighbor as yourself.'" (Matt 22:37–40 NKJV)

Ministry Equipping Assignment. The assignment for this week is a continuation of the task from the previous week. Now that the new believers has been equipped with various tools in order to express and to experience their faith, the challenge is to go forth and become Great Commission Worshippers.

For this final week, the assignment is to fully share the gospel with at least two unbelievers. While this may seem like a difficult task, remember that the new believer has been building relationships over the last five weeks.

This is a time to help the person put all the pieces together. There is a reason for developing salvation and recovery testimonies. The same is true with the development of the active prayer list and the intentional acts of service. All of this, combined with the gospel itself (week 5), helps to create the framework for a *missional/reproducible worshipper.*

Where Do We Go from Here?

It is past time for the church to stop compromising what it means to be a genuine disciple of Christ. This attitude of accepting anything from believers as long as they are involved through weekly church attendance must stop! We must also realize that full obedience to the Great Commission is much more than merely "attracting" people to a building or simply inviting friends to church!

Can a person become a full biblical disciple without experiencing full biblical multiplication through their life as a Christian? In other words, can a person be a true worshipper of Christ if they ignore the commands of the Great Commission to "go" and "make disciples?"

Notice what the apostle Paul says in Eph 4:11–16 (NKJV, italics added):

> And He Himself gave some to be apostles, some prophets, some evangelists, and some pastors and teachers, for the equipping of the saints for the work of ministry, for the edifying of the body of Christ, till we all come to the unity of the faith and of the knowledge of the Son of God, to a perfect man, to the measure of the stature of the fullness of Christ; . . . *speaking the truth in love*, may grow up in all things into Him who is the head— Christ— from whom the whole body, joined and knit together by what every joint supplies, according to the effective working by which every part does its share, causes growth of the body for the edifying of itself in love.

When you combine this call to "equip the saints" with the final commission of Christ in Acts 1:8 to be His "witnesses in Jerusalem and in all Judea and Samaria, and to the end of the earth," the expectation is clear. God fully expects all of His children to multiply! That is why we are called His body. Just as your cells naturally reproduce in order to sustain life and grow, we are commissioned by God to do the same as the church. To accept anything less from so-called believers and call it discipleship is normalizing disobedience to God and tramples on the Great Commission! This kind of approach is naïve at best and will *never* result in creating authentic biblical worshippers.

Unfortunately, I believe that many church leaders have bought into this mind-set that elevates worship as essential to the spiritual life of believers, while evangelism is reserved only for the Green Berets! In the end, these church leaders are setting up their people for spiritual failure. For the sake of attracting crowds, many churches are not only lowering the bar of expectations, they are in fact removing the bar altogether! If the aim is to create a worshipping community, how can that be achieved if believers are allowed to ignore the biblical mandate to reproduce?

Therefore, it is my sincere prayer that we will take a long look at the biblical example of what it means to be an authentic disciple. In doing so, we must stop compartmentalizing the concepts of worship, evangelism, and discipleship. They cannot survive or thrive without each other. Ultimately, there must be an admission that each entity is essential and equally important to creating a genuine follower of Christ. The result will be a fully committed *missional* and *reproducible* worshipper who does not have to be manipulated or enticed to share the "wonders" of God with a hurting and sinful world.

Discussion Questions

1. Explain the disclaimer as it relates to traditional forms of informational discipleship as contrasted with an incarnational approach.

2. Explain the importance of the Great Commandment and worship being the core of the six-week discipleship process.

3. Discuss the *formational* and *transformational* processes as outlined in the first two weeks of the discipleship process.

4. Discuss the *relational* and *missional* processes as outlined in weeks 3 and 4 of the discipleship process.

5. Discuss the importance of the *reproducible* processes as outlined in weeks 5 and 6 of the discipleship process.

CHAPTER 12

The Results of Great Commission Worship

> *Can we really call it worship if it is not followed by service? It is a mockery to praise the Lord inside church walls unless we tell others about Him outside those walls!*

> Hershel Hobbs[1]

One of the most fascinating and intriguing books published during the first decade of the twenty-first century is Malcolm Gladwell's *Outliers*. The author tells a story about extremely successful people and shows how opportunity and legacy impact their lives. Gladwell uses the term *outlier* as a metaphor to demonstrate how culture, family, chance, intellect, and even circumstance can potentially reroute a person's life or career. *Outlier* is a term used in statistics to describe something that is "markedly different in value from the others of a

---

[1] Hershel H. Hobbs, *My Favorite Illustrations* (Nashville: Broadman and Holman, 1990), 272.

sample."[2] Sometimes, an *outlier* is an event that so changes or skews research that the outcome of the test or study turns out differently than expected.

One could say that to the disciples, the resurrection is an *outlier.* It is an unexpected event that forever influenced and changed their lives. Perhaps one could say the Great Commission itself is an outlier or the coming of the Holy Spirit can be seen as something that radically changes the way the disciples think, act, and worship. Certainly, the favor of the Lord upon their lives is something out of the normal everyday routine. Why? Let's take a look at the historical account and find out for ourselves.

The Plan for Worshippers (Acts 1:4-14; 2:1-13)

It is only a few days after His meeting outside of Galilee that Jesus assembles with His disciples once again (Acts 1:4). This time, Jesus develops the strategy for worship evangelism given in Matthew 28 by telling His beloved disciples to be witnesses "in Jerusalem, and in all Judea and Samaria, and to the ends of the earth."

These men of Galilee obey Jesus, stay in Jerusalem, the Holy Spirit comes upon them, and they receive the power of God upon their lives. The disciples are recipients of the power of God. The same power Jesus talks about in Matt 28:18 is now given to the disciples in Acts 2. This power enables the disciples to literally change the world for the kingdom of God. *This is formational worship!*

I remember some years ago watching a television program known as *The A Team*. The plot focused on a commando unit that was sent to prison by a military court for a crime they did not commit. They all escaped from a maximum-security stockade to the Los Angeles underground. This group of socially inept individuals survived as soldiers of fortune. Each week, the plot would demonstrate how "The A Team" solved people's unresolved problems. Each character had rare and special gifts that helped make "The A Team" uniquely

---

[2] Malcolm Gladwell, *Outliers: The Story of Success* (New York: Little, Brown and Company, 2008), 3.

effective. The lead character of the group, Hannibal Smith, was a former military officer played by George Peppard. Near the end of every episode, after a successful and effective strategy, Hannibal Smith would say, "I love it when a plan comes together."

God's plan for Great Commission worship is articulated by the Lord Himself. It includes the scope, supremacy, and mission by which the disciples can take the good news of the gospel to the world. When the Holy Spirit comes upon the disciples in that upper room, it is as if God is saying, "I love it when a plan comes together." When the Holy Spirit comes, God reinforces the idea that His master plan is still intact. That plan is to reveal Himself to all men and women everywhere.

Our response to this revelation?

Transformational worship! God changes us, and we worship yet again. This is exactly what happened that day in the upper room. The disciples experienced worship that forever transformed their lives.

The Provision for Worship (Acts 2:42–47)

As these new Christians take on the extraordinary role of "sharing the good news," they praise God with the favor of the people from all nations, walks of life, and professions. Apparently, they leave a very impressive testimony through their worship, work, and witness. They devote themselves to teaching, fellowship, breaking of the bread (sacraments or communion), and prayer (Acts 2:42). They respect established traditions as much as possible and meet in the temple and synagogue:

> The apostles were doing many miracles and signs, and everyone felt great respect for God. All the believers were together and shared everything. They would sell their land and the things they owned and then divide the money and give it to anyone who needed it. The believers met together in the Temple every day. They ate together in their homes, happy to share their food with joyful hearts. They praised God and were liked by all the people.

Every day the Lord added those who were being saved to the group of believers. (Acts 2:43-47 NCV)

Thousands of people become worshippers of Jesus Christ. In the process, God provides miracles and signs, unity, food and shelter, and favor—approval from God and great esteem with people. The harvest of new worshippers is a daily routine. The fire of revival experienced by the coming of the Holy Spirit spreads throughout the known world. God chooses to bless the young church through the work and ministry of committed Great Commission Worshippers.

The Promise of God Is Fulfilled
(Acts 3–4:13,28,31–33; 5:41)

Remember, there are two powers in the earth, the power of God and the power of Satan, and there is eternal hostility between the two. In the words of A. W. Tozer:

> Satan is aflame with desire for unlimited dominion over the human family; and whenever that evil ambition is challenged by the Spirit of God, he invariably retaliates with savage fury. It is possible within the provisions of redemptive grace to enter into a state of union with Christ so perfect that the world will instinctively react toward us exactly as it did toward Him in the days of His flesh. It is the Spirit of Christ in us that will draw Satan's fire. The people of the world will not much care what we believe and they will stare vacantly at our religious forms, but there is one thing they will never forgive us—the presence of God's Spirit in our hearts. They may not know the cause of that strange feeling of antagonism which rises within them, but it will be nonetheless real and dangerous. Satan will never cease to make war on the Man-child, and the soul in which dwells the Spirit of Christ will continue to be the target for his attacks.[3]

---

[3] A. W. Tozer, *The Warfare of the Spirit* (Camp Hill, PA: Christian Publications, Inc.), 3–4.

It is about 3:00 p.m. when a crippled man sitting at the temple gate sees the apostles and asks for food and money. Peter looks at the man and says, "Silver and gold I do not have, but what I do have I give you: In the name of Jesus Christ of Nazareth, rise up and walk" (Acts 3:6 NKJV). Instantly, the man begins to walk. Crippled since birth, now, at the age of 40, he experiences the healing power of Jesus.

As one can imagine, this caused quite a stir. In a few minutes thousands of people gathered at Solomon's porch—outside the temple. Peter takes the opportunity and preaches the gospel. He proclaims "Jesus as the only way to heaven." He tells the people standing in front of that temple porch that Jesus has risen from the dead, and he proclaims that they can have eternal life—only through Jesus. Peter and John give credit for this man's healing to Jesus. These two men openly and unashamedly glorify God for all that has been accomplished in this man's life.

The religious leaders are threatened by the preaching of the good news of Christ. They take Peter and John and throw them into prison. The next morning, they bring the disciples before a makeshift court. After some time and debate, they dismiss Peter and John from their presence. In the middle of Satan's attack, there is an incredible testimony from the lips of these evil Sadducees about the disciples (Acts 4:12–13,28). Even in the midst of extreme persecution, Satan cannot stop the power of God. Even during a period of trial and total misrepresentation of the truth by those seeking to destroy the work of these two men, God allows His name to be blessed and glorified. So much so, the disciples, once freed from prison, rejoice in the Lord because they are counted worthy enough to endure persecution for the sake of God's kingdom and the testimony of Jesus Christ. They are living *missional worship.*

What happens here is what can happen in your life and mine. We can see the results of lives committed to being Great Commission Worshippers. Look at what the unsaved community witnesses taking place in the lives of these men:

First, *they acknowledge that Peter and John are men of courage.* This is the same Peter who denied Christ. God has miraculously changed these men into men of bravery, audacity, and valor. They no longer hide behind their leader and wait for an appropriate time to speak. These men stand up with boldness and proclaim the day of the Lord without fear of man. The secret? The Holy Spirit has empowered both of these men. Jesus has delivered on His promise, and these men are forever transformed. The same thing can happen to you and me.

Second, the Sadducees concede that *God uses ordinary men who had been with Jesus to influence and impact the world with the gospel*. God loves taking the ordinary and transforming them into extra-ordinary vessels for use in His service. He often uses the most unlikely to carry out His purposes. These two brothers, filled with the Holy Spirit, looked like ordinary, run-of-the-mill fishermen. But, when Peter and John spoke the name of Jesus, a man crippled from birth was miraculously healed. These Great Commission Worshippers preached the gospel with clarity, and thousands became worshippers in one day. And, God wants to place His blessing on you and me. He still takes ordinary people, just like you and me, and uses them to do His work.

Third, the religious leaders give testimony that *they had been with Jesus*. This is perhaps the greatest declaration of the outward evidence of an inward working in a person's life. *Everyone*, including the religious leaders who were seeking to marginalize and destroy the influence of Jesus on their community, knew Peter and John had been with Jesus. He had radically changed them, and the markings were forever placed on their lives. When men and women have been with Jesus, the power of the gospel is manifested for others to see. As we spend time with Jesus, the Holy Spirit equips us, and people observe a difference in our lives.

Fourth, they admitted that *Peter and John were men of prayer and it was evidence that the power of God was upon them*. Apparently, these disciples were not at all bashful about praying in public (or, for that matter, publicly [and privately] praying whenever the Holy Spirit prompted). They were constantly in a mind to pray. That is what happens when ordinary men do extraordinary things in the power of God. They pray. They stay constantly plugged in to their source for power. "Nothing of eternal consequence is ever accomplished apart from prayer."[4]

Fifth, *the unsaved recognize that the power of God is upon these men*. Jesus told His disciples that He was the recipient of all power in heaven and earth. Now, we see that power given to the disciples. This is extraordinary power for an extraordinary time. It is strength beyond reason or understanding. This power just cannot be explained apart from the work of God. The disciples already know it is God's power that gives them the ability to do great and mighty things. But, the testimony of this power is so great that those who do not claim to be followers of Christ even acknowledge it as a supernatural gift from God.

Sixth, the religious leaders realize that *Peter and John spoke the Word of God boldly and were unified by the gospel*. Isn't it amazing how the power of God provides a sense of boldness for doing the work of God? There are a hidden strength, intestinal fortitude, and empowerment that only God gives. It is this same boldness that Moses experienced when standing before Pharaoh. God granted this kind of boldness to a shepherd boy, David, when standing before the giant. It is this same sense of boldness that Elijah demonstrated that day on Mount Carmel when, as the Spirit of God was upon Elijah, he confronted and defeated more than 400 prophets of Baal. It is this boldness that characterizes the apostle Paul when he stands on Mars Hill and proclaims the truth about the unknown god. It is this same boldness that enables the disciples to stand before rulers and kings and proclaim the gospel without fear. And, it is *this same boldness* that God wants to give you and me as Great Commission Worshippers. God doesn't give us a spirit of fear. Rather, God gives us a spirit of bold confidence that only comes when we walk and work with the power of God on our lives.

Seventh, these Sadducees see that Peter, John, and *all the believers are in one heart*. Worship of God unifies. When we are in unity, in one heart, we are able to focus on Jesus. When we focus on worshipping

---

[4] Jerry Falwell in convocation at Liberty University, May 2, 2007.

Jesus—serving Him with all our heart, loving Him with passion, and living for Him without constraint—our motives are unified, our methods are organized, and our mission is realized. Jesus prays in John 17 that these disciples will have unity so that "the world may know that you sent me and loved them even as you loved me" (John 17:23 ESV). They were in one accord when the Holy Spirit came upon them in Acts 2, and God shows His blessing upon these believers by giving them unity.

Eighth, it is obvious to these unsaved accusers that Peter and John *testify to the power of God*. They do not bend to the temptation of ego and self-interest. These devoted followers recognize that what they have is from God. They unashamedly give all the credit for every accomplishment to Jesus with boldness, reverence, and full faith. They proclaim their power in the name of Jesus. And, the world stands and watches as Jesus is glorified through the lives of obedient believers. The power of God is evidenced in all that is accomplished.

Ninth, the unsaved see that *God's grace is upon them*. This is the kind of grace that puts into action the principles we studied in Rom 12:1–2. It influences and shapes our attitudes about God, about ourselves, about ministry, and about others and their gifts. People see this grace in our lives because it impacts our behavior. Quoting the apostle Paul from Romans:

> Do not think of yourself more highly than you ought. . . . Love must be sincere. . . . Never be lacking in zeal . . . but keep your spiritual fervor, serving the Lord, Be joyful in hope, patient in affliction, faithful in prayer. Do not be proud, but be willing to associate with people of low position. Do not be conceited. . . .
> Do not commit adultery, do not murder, do not steal, do not covet, . . . love your neighbor as yourself. (Rom 12:3,9,11–12,26; 13:9 NIV)

Tenth, perhaps the thing the Sadducees resent most is that Peter and John *enjoy the favor of the people*. They examine every aspect of their lives and find that Peter and John are above reproach. It is not until these religious leaders realize the favor of the people is swinging toward the disciples that legal action is finally taken. They are horrified with the idea that believers in Jesus change the world. Peter and John experience *reproducible worship.* They are able to see the worship they experience on a daily basis reproduced in the lives of hundreds, of thousands of people around them.

How will these principles play out in our lives?

First, our worship and evangelism should be executed *with focused intentionality.* If we are going to experience the kind of favor from the Lord these early Christians enjoyed, our worship of God and labor of evangelism must be done with one intentional purpose—to glorify God. We must be preoccupied with God. Our worship habits, work ethic, evangelistic endeavors, and kingdom building must begin with deliberate, planned, premeditated intention.

Robert J. Morgan tells the story about a man who dreamed that an angel escorted him to church one Sunday.

> There he saw the keyboard musician playing vigorously, praise team singing, the musicians playing their instruments with gusto. But the man heard no sound. The congregation was singing, but the sound was utterly muted. When the minister rose to speak, his lips moved, but there was no volume. In amazement, the man turned to his escort for an explanation.
>
> "This is the way it sounds to us in heaven," said the angel. "You hear nothing because there is nothing to hear. These people are engaged in the form of worship, but their thoughts are on other things and their hearts are far away."[5]

If we are doing all we do with the spirit of intentionality, our thoughts, motives, attitudes, and activities will reflect the glory of God. While we will thrill at the reality of God's blessings, the credit of success will go to God alone. Karen Burton Mains expresses that principle this way:

> In truth, if Christ were bodily present and we could see Him with more than our soul's eyes, all our worship would become

---

[5] Robert J. Morgan, *Preacher's Sourcebook of Creative Sermon Illustrations* (Nashville: Thomas Nelson, 2007), 809.

intentional. If Christ stood on our platforms, we would bend our knees without asking. If He stretched out His hands and we saw the wounds, our hearts would break; we would confess our sins and weep over our shortcomings. If we could hear His voice leading the hymns, we too would sing heartily; the words would take on meaning. The Bible reading would be lively; meaning would pierce to the marrow of our souls. If Christ walked our aisles, we would hasten to make amends with that brother or sister to whom we had not spoken. We would volunteer for service; the choir loft would be crowded. If we knew Christ would attend our church Sunday after Sunday, the front pews would fill fastest, believers would arrive early, offering plates would be laden with sacrificial but gladsome gifts, prayers would concentrate our attention. Yet, Christ is present.[6]

Second, our worship and evangelistic efforts should be executed *with humility and surrender.* Humility comes as we give credit for any success to God and God alone. Remember, the ancient preacher reminds us of the principle as applied to our own achievements, victories, and accomplishments: "Let another praise you," he says, "and not your own mouth; someone else, and not your own lips" (Prov 27:2 NIV).

The third lesson we have learned from our study of Great Commission worship involves our own understanding of eternity. Our worship and evangelism efforts must be accomplished *with eternity in view.* Robert J. Morgan's documentation of Edward Kimball's meager attempt at evangelism provides apt illustration to this principle:

Edward Kimball was determined to win his Sunday school class to Christ. A teenager named Dwight Moody tended to fall asleep on Sundays, but Kimball, undeterred, set out to reach him at work. His heart was pounding as he entered the store where the young man worked. "I put my hand on his shoulder, and as I leaned over I placed my foot upon a shoebox. I asked him to come to Christ." But Kimball left thinking he had botched the

---

[6] Karen Burton Mains, *Sing Joyfully* (Carol Stream, IL: Tabernacle, 1989), 3–6.

job. Moody, however, left the store that day a new person and eventually became the most prominent evangelist in America.

On June 17, 1873, Moody arrived in Liverpool, England, for a series of crusades. Moody visited a Baptist chapel pastured by a scholarly man named F. B. Meyer. At Moody's invitation, Meyer toured America. At Northfield Bible Conference, he challenged the crowds, saying, "If you are not willing to give up everything for Christ, are you willing to be made willing?" That remark changed the life of a struggling young minister named J. Wilbur Chapman.

Chapman proceeded to become a powerful traveling evangelist in the early 1900's, and he recruited a converted baseball player named Billy Sunday. Under Chapman's eye, Sunday became one of the most spectacular evangelists in American history. His campaign in Charlotte, North Carolina, produced a group of converts who continued praying for another such visitation of the Spirit. In 1934, they invited evangelist Mordecai Ham to conduct a citywide crusade. On October 8th, Ham, discouraged, wrote a prayer to God on the stationary of his Charlotte hotel: "Lord, give us a Pentecost here. Pour out thy Spirit tomorrow."

His prayer was answered beyond his dreams when a Central High School student name Billy Graham gave his heart to Jesus.

And Edward Kimball thought he had botched the job![7]

At the end of the day, the church does not need another song book, worship set, worship video, or praise team standing out in front of a screaming group of young people leading the latest songs about God. The church does not need another event or goal-driven evangelism program simply for the sake of filling up our precious time with things to do.

---

[7] Robert J. Morgan, *On This Day: 365 Amazing and Inspiring Stories about Saints, Martyrs and Heroes* (Nashville: Thomas Nelson, 1997), June 17.

The church needs—and God is seeking—men and women totally devoted to Him, full of love for God because of what Christ has done on the cross, transformed by the work of the Holy Spirit in their lives, and passionately motivated by their worship to tell the good news of Jesus Christ to everyone they meet. What the church needs are men and women who want to make a difference in the lives of people for eternity. What the church needs is men and women who live and breathe Great Commission worship. They have experienced formational, transformational, relational, missional, and reproducible worship. They see the Great Commission through hearts of worship. They live worship for the glory of God and the testimony of Jesus Christ.

To Him be the glory and the dominion forever and ever. Amen.
(1 Pet 5:11 NKJV)

Discussion Questions

1. List and discuss the basic steps to becoming a biblical Great Commission Worshipper.

2. Based on your reading in the previous chapters, and outlined in this chapter, which step is most challenging to you? Why?

3. Some people might say that worship and evangelism have nothing to do with each other. How do you respond after reading this book? Back up your response with Scripture.

4. Is it fair to expect every believer to become a Great Commission Worshipper? If so, how will that look in your life on a daily basis?

5. When it says in this chapter that "our worship and evangelism efforts must be accomplished with eternity in view," what do you think the author means? How does this impact your becoming a Great Commission Worshipper?

Subject Index

Scripture Index

131024